Law, Necessity, and the Crisis of the State

This book contains the first English translations of Santi Romano's important essays, 'On the Decree Laws and the State of Siege During the Earthquakes in Messina and Reggio Calabria' (1909) and 'The Modern State and its Crisis' (1910).

Before Santi Romano wrote his masterpiece *The Legal Order* in 1917–18, he lay the foundations for his ground-breaking theory of law in these two essays, which are still central to scholarly debates about his legacy. The main focus of 'On the Decree Laws' is the concept of necessity as a source of law. Such a controversial view anticipated the much more renowned conception of the state of exception advanced later by Carl Schmitt in his *Political Theology* and has provided a reference point for Giorgio Agamben. The second essay, 'The Modern State and its Crisis', is concerned with the emergence of social forces that the early 20th-century administrative state was struggling to tame. Pursuing an insight that he would develop in *The Legal Order*, Romano argued that a solution could be found in a public law theory that was able to reconcile the need for a shared constitutional frame with the internal orderings of nonstate movements.

Indispensable for contemporary scholars to understand how Romano's most revolutionary notions came about, as well as to fully appreciate the theoretical import of his concept of law, this book will appeal to legal and political theorists and others who are interested in how law deals and should deal with emergencies and social crises.

Mariano Croce is Associate Professor of Political Philosophy at the Department of Philosophy of Sapienza – Università di Roma, Italy.

LAW AND POLITICS: CONTINENTAL PERSPECTIVES

series

series editors
Mariano Croce, *Sapienza University of Rome, Italy*
Marco Goldoni, *University of Glasgow, UK*

for information about the series and details of previous and forthcoming titles, see https://www.routledge.com/Law-and-Politics/book-series/LPCP

A GlassHouse book

Law, Necessity, and the Crisis of the State
The Early Writings of Santi Romano

**Edited and Translated by
Mariano Croce**

a GlassHouse book

English language translation © 2023 Mariano Croce

First published 2023
by Routledge
4 Park Square, Milton Park, Abingdon, Oxon OX14 4RN

and by Routledge
605 Third Avenue, New York, NY 10158

a GlassHouse book

Routledge is an imprint of the Taylor & Francis Group, an informa business

The right of Mariano Croce to be identified as editor and translator of this work has been asserted in accordance with sections 77 and 78 of the Copyright, Designs and Patents Act 1988.

All rights reserved. No part of this book may be reprinted or reproduced or utilised in any form or by any electronic, mechanical, or other means, now known or hereafter invented, including photocopying and recording, or in any information storage or retrieval system, without permission in writing from the publishers.

Trademark notice: Product or corporate names may be trademarks or registered trademarks, and are used only for identification and explanation without intent to infringe.

British Library Cataloguing-in-Publication Data
A catalogue record for this book is available from the British Library

Library of Congress Cataloging-in-Publication Data
A catalog record has been requested for this book

ISBN: 978-1-032-38968-4 (hbk)
ISBN: 978-1-032-38969-1 (pbk)
ISBN: 978-1-003-34777-4 (ebk)

DOI: 10.4324/9781003347774

Typeset in Times New Roman
by Taylor & Francis Books

Contents

Santi Romano before legal institutionalism: The order
above and beyond positive law   1
MARIANO CROCE

1   On the Decree Laws and the State of Siege During the
Earthquakes in Messina and Reggio Calabria   24

2   The Modern State and its Crisis   50

Bibliography   66
Index   68

Santi Romano before legal institutionalism

The order above and beyond positive law

Mariano Croce

All those who lend themselves to the study of Santi Romano's jurisprudence and intellectual legacy are required to perform a sort of initiation ritual, something that readers will find in almost all texts about him. Romano scholars somewhat feel a compulsion to take sides on the vexed question of how genuine his legal pluralism was, and conversely, how much he remained loyal to a picture of legal reality where the state still hovers over all other legal and non-legal entities. A particular step in this ritual is the conjuring of Norberto Bobbio's self-reassuring sentence that 'Romano was a pluralist from a theoretical standpoint, but a monist from an ideological one.'[1] In the face of it, interpreters part ways. Those who advocate Romano's innovative view of legal reality as one that includes but is not dominated by the state confront those who draw attention to his intermittent opinion that the state is and should remain the fundamental legal entity, one that can include others but should never cease to be the institution *of*, rather than *among*, institutions. As we will see, the two essays translated in this book nicely expose such a seeming contradiction. At some junctures, Romano appears to be utterly prepared to do away, if not with the state, with its normative pre-eminence. Yet, at other junctures, he is adamant that the state is the platform on which other normative entities can negotiate the terms of their coexistence. There is no need for quotations here, as I will get back to the issue time and again in this introductory writing.

While the following pages are intended to contextualize Romano's two essays, the thrust of my argument will be that the prism of *theoretical pluralism vs. state ideology* neglects the main outcome of his jurisprudential endeavour. As we will see, there is no denying that in

---

1 N. Bobbio, *Dalla struttura alla funzione. Dalla struttura alla funzione* (Roma-Bari: Laterza, 2007), 154.

DOI: 10.4324/9781003347774-1

2 Santi Romano before legal institutionalism

both these texts, as well as in many others, Romano teeters between extolling sources of law other than state-based ones and insisting that they should be brought within the scope of the constitutional order. However, this is not anywhere near a friction, let alone a contradiction. Rather, his ongoing oscillations are part and parcel of his persisting effort to identify an area within which legal entities can negotiate (though this latter is not a term of Romano's). A correlated objective of this introduction will be to foreground the vital link that exists between the two essays. 'On the Decree-laws and the State of Siege on the Occasion of the Messina and Reggio-Calabria Earthquake' (hereinafter 'On the Decree-laws') and 'The Modern State and its Crisis' (hereinafter 'The Modern State'), respectively published in 1909 and 1910, seem to touch on different themes and hence to pursue distinct objectives. Yet, I will make the case that they are the laboratory of the monumental theory Romano developed nine years from then in *The Legal Order* (1917–18),[2] a milestone in the tradition of classic legal institutionalism and, well beyond that, a major jurisprudential achievement of the 20th century. This obviously does not imply that the 1909–1910 essays are preparatory sketches for the grand theory to come. Quite the contrary, in these writings readers will find invaluable theoretical lines that make sense of a unitary project which got off the ground at the turn of the century and was not completed until 1947 with Romano's last book, *Frammenti di un dizionario giuridico* (*Fragments of a Legal Dictionary*).[3]

To summarize the argument that I will put forward in the subsequent sections, 'On the Decree-laws' and 'The Modern State' deal with two critical issues in the general theory of law and the state, as well as in the concrete historical circumstances of the early 20th century and still haunt our present, as the events of the last two decades have sadly reminded us. These are, on the one hand, the occurrence of serious emergencies that require temporarily enhancing the executive to the disadvantage of the legislative and the judiciary powers; on the other hand, the rise of associations and organizations that claimed administrative and jurisdictional autonomy to the disadvantage of the

---

2 S. Romano, *The Legal Order* (Abingdon: Routledge, 2017). On the conceptual and historical connection between 'The Modern State' and *The Legal Order*, see A. Romano, 'Santi Romano, *Lo Stato moderno e la sua crisi* e *L'ordinamento giuridico*' (2011) 2 *Rivista trimestrale di diritto pubblico* 333–358, and P. Grossi, '*Lo Stato moderno e la sua crisi* (a cento anni dalla prolusione pisana di Santi Romano)' (2011) 1 *Rivista trimestrale di diritto pubblico* 1–22.

3 S. Romano, *Frammenti di un dizionario giuridico* (Macerata: Quodlibet, 2019).

state's authority. These issues seem to go down different roads. 'On the Decree-laws' addresses how the state should react to emergencies that make state law inapplicable to a specific context. The need for emergency powers raises the question of what happens when state laws prove inapplicable to a particular territory or area of social life. 'The Modern State' tells a different story. It dwells on the progressive erosion of the late 19th-century normative ideal of the state-person as the sole source of legality and the emergence of normative bodies that were posing a threat to the unity of the state. So, on one side, the expansion of the state authority; on the other, its contraction.

But it is exactly when one disposes of the state vs. nonstate dichotomy that the connection between these issues comes to light. And one of Romano's main virtues is the ability to escape the tight clench of this false bifurcation. The sudden materialization of conditions where ordinary laws are inapplicable, just like the conditions in which nonstate normative entities disavow state law, unveils something that is the core of his theorizing: even in *prima facie* chaotic and unstable circumstances where conditions for orderly interactions seem to deteriorate dramatically, an underlying order is at work, however invisible and silent it may be. This conclusion must have come as a shock for a jurist like Romano who, as I will discuss, was immovable about the supreme virtues of the state-person. But it is in the first decade of the 20th century that he came to acknowledge that his deliberate intention to rescue state law could hardly take its cue from the belief that state law is the beginning and the end of legal life. In a way that would subvert one hundred years of jurisprudential inquiry, Romano penetrated the recesses of legal reality, those that are only visible in rare and hazardous circumstances, to demonstrate that the social is always and already organized. In other words, even when the concreteness of social and political conditions only displays disorder and confusion, there is inescapably some order at work, even if it is almost invisible. This is the spark that ignited the ten-year rumination which culminated in *The Legal Order*. But to figure out what this implies, it is imperative to make a few preliminary steps into 'On the Decree-laws' and 'The Modern State.'

Background concerns

Romano's formation as a jurist took place in Palermo, one of the centres of an Italian jurisprudential renaissance, in the last decade of the 19th century. Undoubtedly, those were the years of the celebration of the state as the alpha and omega of the law. What today is known as state monism was an unquestioned premise of legal studies in both the

4   Santi Romano before legal institutionalism

public and private fields, so much so that the public and the state were believed to coincide with one another. Though very young, Romano showed remarkable knowledge of the German theory of public law, as well as German legal theory in general. This should not be underrated, if it is true that it was 19th-century German jurisprudence that first produced a theorization of the state entirely and exclusively based on juristic categories. In Italy, Romano's supervisor and guide, Vittorio Emanuele Orlando (1860–1952) gave way to the foundation of a new theory of administrative law with the same grandiose aspiration in the last decades of the 19th century. He was on the lookout for fresh grounds for the science of the public, as he thought that public law, compared to private law, suffered a conspicuous lack of appropriate categories and systematic knowledge. While private lawyers could count on firm mastery of key concepts like property, contract, obligation, and so on, public lawyers fidgeted with concepts that derived their origin from other disciplines and had been elaborated with political and ideological objectives, such as state, sovereignty, and government. A purely legal treatment of those public-law concepts would pave the way, Orlando thought, for a genuinely legal science of public powers and the administrative state, freed from the speculations of philosophy and political ideologies. The model had to be the jurists' activity in the field of private law, as they marked off the boundaries of a science that was able to identify the concrete objects of its knowledge.[4]

Drawing the boundaries of legal science was no facetious accomplishment, as it was basically meant to secure the autonomy of jurisprudence as a science from other disciplines as well as political power. And this should not go unnoticed when it comes to Romano's thinking, as he is claimed to be one of the scholars who advocated flexing the stiff boundaries of public law to make room for new social forces that were demanding political and jurisdictional autonomy from the state. Most of all, substate groups, associations, and organizations felt dissatisfied with the parliamentary system as it was unable to represent their interests.[5] For these interests were inherently *collective*, in the sense that they could not be broken down into the interests of their individual members. Importantly, at the end of the 19th century, radical ideologies had infiltrated many of these groups. Ideals of revolutionary

---

4   See M. Fioravanti, *La scienza del diritto pubblico. Dottrine dello Stato e della Costituzione tra Otto e Novecento* (Milano: Giuffrè, 2001) 3–63.
5   See C. Magnani, 'Stato e rappresentanza politica nel pensiero giuridico di Orlando e Romano' (2000) 2 *Materiali per una storia della cultura giuridica* 349–386.

syndicalism, socialism, and anarchism were spreading among groups that came to consider armed revolution as an option, however radical. Even more worryingly for those who cherished the constitutional order in peril, revolutionary groups were able to win sympathy from the more moderate ones, as the activity of the former did prove able to alter the political scenario for the better.

In this light, the idea that Romano intended to make room for the normative bodies of these groups within state law, however correct it may be, is to be clarified in full detail. Certainly, as I will illustrate in the subsequent section, he thought these groups could not be straight-forwardly ignored by the state legal order. This would result in a costly mistake for the state in the first place, as those groups' vociferous agitation was the symptom of a real crisis of the state-form. However, Romano also believed that negotiation could not take place within the field of parliamentary politics. It could only occur within the field of a renewed public law. This is a point one should bear in mind if one is to penetrate the meanders of his project. To elucidate this, it is worth conjuring Nicola Matteucci's pointy criticism to Romano's alleged social sensitivity. Matteucci noted that it is an error to think that the project of classic legal institutionalists, and above all Romano's, was to open new spaces for 'society' and that, on the contrary, 'today we should flip over the criticism addressed to Romano, viz., that he turned the law into society. Rather, he laid the foundations for juridifying society as a whole, and this prevented studying the latter with a more appropriate methodology.'[6] This is a piercing remark, in that Romano's strategy was in fact one that intended to present the legal field as the only venue where group antagonism could be turned into virtuous cooperation. Certainly, this implied an intensifying juridification of the social, as I will discuss, and a devaluation of politics as the principal instrument of social mediation.

With a terminology that was not Romano's, one could say that he was trying to mark off and purify a *juristic point of view* as a *technique of composition*. This is a vantage point where strictly juristic categories allow describing society with both transformative and reparative effects. If this is the key to reading Romano – admittedly, my own key – let us first examine based on what he arrived at this conclusion. In the first years of the 20th century, and even before, his studies were nurtured by three firm convictions. First, he considered the British constitutional model to be preferable to the French one because of the former's extraordinary

---

6   N. Matteucci, 'Positivismo giuridico e costituzionalismo' (1963) 3 *Rivista trimestrale di diritto e procedura civile* 985–1100, at 1029, fn. 81.

6 Santi Romano before legal institutionalism

flexibility and ductility – although he was aware that it was inapplicable to other historical traditions.[7] Second, in the footsteps of Savigny and the German historical school of jurisprudence, he thought the legislator's capacity to interpret a historical tradition and to draw juristic resources from it was limited, to say the least. Third, he was certain that the legislative state of the 19th century was destined to morph into the administrative state, where juristic knowledge combined with a reformed corpus of public and administrative law would provide a steadier basis for a growingly complex society.

By reading Romano's texts between 1901 and 1909, one can easily see how dubious he grew about the potentials of public law in its existing form. Despite this, he was adamant that the road that would take from the legislative to the administrative state was paved. Therefore, he concluded that the most effective way to accelerate this process, as well as to domesticate the growing dissatisfaction of substate groups, was the complete revision of the categories and the lexicon of public law. While he thought Continental constitutional models and the representative system centred on the legislature could do little or nothing, the way out was not the demolition of the state and its legal structure. Rather, it was necessary to provide the state legal order with workable and updated juristic instruments. From this vantage point, it is all the more clear that Romano never yielded to sociological inclinations[8] – if by this we mean an uncomplicated openness to non-legal practices and the normativity they engender. As we will see, Matteucci's remark is well-placed: Romano took the other way, as he strove to subsume all instances of social normativity under legal normativity, to the extent that in his jurisprudence there is no conceptually justifiable boundary left between the legal and the non-legal. As I will insist, this

---

7 See C. Pinelli, 'La costituzione di Santi Romano e i primi Maestri dell'età repubblicana' (2012) 3 *Rivista Italiana per le Scienze Giuridiche* 179–225, particularly 181–182.

8 Against this interpretation, see M. Cascavilla, 'Santi Romano e la concezione sociologica del diritto' (2020) 1 *Sociologia del diritto* 9–23. The author argues that Romano did try to accommodate the socio-historical events that were taking place before his eyes at the level of his legal theory. Cascavilla recognizes that Romano's attention to the relations between the state and social forces is party to the need for a more adequate theory of law, and yet identifies genuine traces that bring his institutionalism back into the sphere of the sociology of law. I seek to explain why this interpretation, however suggestive, is misplaced in M. Croce, 'Istituire il sociale: Santi Romano e Karl Llewellyn sulla tecnica del diritto' (2022) *Teoria e storia del diritto privato* 1–20. I need not summarize my argument here, as I broached the issue by building and commenting on Matteucci's remark.

Santi Romano before legal institutionalism   7

is much more than the law's openness to the social, because the social is entirely dispersed into the legal. It was a deft move, one that would certainly make the law the only discipline that could preside over the patterns of exchange, interaction, conflict, and negotiation among groups and their normative background. However, it was not until 1917/18 that Romano made this conceptual strategy explicit. In the essays translated in this book, this is an unstated, mostly unaware theoretical premise that still needs specifying. Yet, it bears keeping it in mind, lest the gist of his reasoning get lost. Now, it is about time to make a few steps into the two essays.

Why should the state survive?

Originally 'The Modern State' was the inaugural address of the academic year 1909/10 at the University of Pisa. Romano came to Pisa in 1908 as a professor of constitutional law after teaching international law and then constitutional law at the University of Modena. Prior to that date, he was an extremely promising young jurist who had dealt with a variety of constitutional and administrative issues, such as subjective public rights and the nature of constitutional bodies, administrative jurisdiction, conflicts of competence, and so on. Interestingly enough, he had so far never taken issue with the conditions and the future of political institutions. However, the pressing questions that were causing social and political distress could not evade the brilliance of a one-of-a-kind scholar. As I hinted, at the turn of the century, the issues to cope with for the state structure were many and serious. The recent enlargement of suffrage was followed by the expansion of the administrative apparatus and public services, the increase in the number of public agencies, and new forms of public service management. Meanwhile, the expansion of the education system and social legislation, as well as the growing role of the state to govern labour disputes, in an age where trade unions were thriving from the left to the centre through to the right.

That which came as a shocking wake-up call was the development of trade unionism inside the administration. A growing number of civil servants adhered to a union. By 1903, the many federations of public employees merged into the Confederation of Public and Private Administrative Employees. A general strike had been called in 1904. At the end of it, the President of the Council of Ministers Giovanni Giolitti asked and obtained from the King the dissolution of the Chambers and new elections to take more effective measures with the new government. But further agitation and strikes would follow. The

8 Santi Romano before legal institutionalism

unions advocated radical innovations such as shaking hierarchies, forming technical parliaments, involving the employees in the management of public services. Whereas the unionism from the left, even the most radical and violent, was understandable and probably controllable, now the enemy was penetrating the organs of the state.[9]

It is important to note that these phenomena were mostly addressed, especially by political scientists, as the demise of sovereignty, the end of parliamentarism, and the comeback of medieval feudalism. This was not Romano's take, though. Quite the reverse, he was downright hostile to that account since he thought it could even make the situation worse. And this explains the beginning of 'The Modern State,' where Romano gnaws at political and sociological theories that described the existing scenario in terms of a clash between political entities pursuing incompatible objectives: the autonomy of substate groups vs. the unity of the state. And he also excoriates those who corroborated this account of the social environment by offering an image of law as a mere matter of power, whereby the law is alleged to be nothing but what is imposed by the most powerful. Against this conception, Romano conjures von Savigny's spirit and wisdom. And his conjuring is especially important to understand what he is getting at: hardly ever can the law be reduced to its actual manifestations, whether or not power is involved – as most often is, when it comes to establishing an order. In this sense, in these initial pages von Savigny is the juristic deity symbolizing the irreducibility of law to matters of fact. The law is first and foremost matter of knowledge, as I will detail.[10]

---

9   See S. Cassese, 'La prolusione romaniana sulla crisi dello Stato moderno e il suo tempo' (2012) 1 *Le Carte e la Storia* 5–8; A. Morrone, 'Per il metodo del costituzionalista: riflettendo su 'Lo Stato moderno e la sua crisi' di Santi Romano' (2012) 2 *Quaderni costituzionali* 369–390; M. Dogliani, 'La fortuna della teoria romaniana dell'ordinamento nelle varie aree disciplinari: diritto costituzionale' (2018) 3 *Diritto pubblico* 873–904.

10 Needless to say, Savigny's and Romano's objectives and theoretical strategy do not easily map onto each other. More than anything Savigny emphasized the importance of the historical tradition for understanding law (as opposed to the abstract and universalistic discourse of natural law theories). Put otherwise, Savigny aimed to overcome the apparent contradiction between legal normativity and historical fact. For Savigny, historical knowledge, i.e., the jurist's grasping the (evolution) of the guiding principles of Roman law, rather than technical expertise, was central to understanding and further developing (German) law. Romano was obviously not concerned with Roman law and how it could yield principles for producing new law. His notion of technical expertise related to the jurist's solid grasp of the basic principles of public law at its highest. In this sense, the figure of Savigny plays the same role it does in another

Santi Romano before legal institutionalism 9

From this we can get a sense of Romano's theoretical strategy: it behoves the law to provide a description of social reality that does not twist the opposition into a conflict destined to be ended by the annihilation of one of the conflicting parties. The idea of a conflict between factions advancing opposed claims is an oversimplification. He continues by remarking that the construction of the state in the 19th century was principled on the same type of mistake: a simplified conception of social and legal reality. Along the lines of erstwhile critiques of the French Revolution and its aftermath, he argues that the revolutionists took a saw to the branch they were sitting on. While the Revolution was nurtured by the uncontainable discontent of groups that would not see their interests met within the structure of the Ancien Régime, its main produce turned out to be an untenable vision of the constitutional order as based on two fundamental entities: the individual with its subjective rights and the state with its sovereignty. This was a fatal mistake that would be a nail in the coffin of the moribund constitutional order of the 19th century, in that it left no space for recognizing other legal actors that were not reducible to either the individual or the state. In both cases, subsequent to the French Revolution and one century after, when new social ferments were bursting out, a miscalculation was posing a serious threat to any reform strategy, that is, oversimplification. Reality was much more complex than the conceptual tapestry of the 19th-century legislative state admitted.[11]

The complexity view that Romano was advocating required, as I alluded, new juristic categories that could account for a reality in need of proper verbalization. These groups, according to him, should be put in the condition to acquire speakability, as it were, within the boundaries and through the categories of state public law. This explains his gradually moving towards the institutional theory of 1917 – something that most probably in 1909 he was already fantasizing about. Be this as it may, in 'The Modern State' his firm point was that public law theory should provide *juristic* categories capable of identifying the *essentially legal* nature of the ongoing opposition. Doubtless, he thought that only the state could count on such a rich repository of legal knowledge that

key jurisprudential essay, Carl Schmitt's 'The Plight of European Jurisprudence' ((1990) 83 *Telos* 35–70), where he developed his peculiar juristic institutionalism. On this latter type of institutionalism and the role of jurisprudence, see Croce, Salvatore, *Carl Schmitt's Institutional Theory*, (Cambridge: Cambridge University Press, 2022), Chap. 7.

11 See A. Sandulli, 'Santi Romano and the Perception of the Public Law Complexity' (2009) 1 *Italian Journal of Public Law* 1–38.

10 *Santi Romano before legal institutionalism*

hardly anybody else could carry out the job.[12] This is why he staunchly held onto the state as the main legal actor on stage.[13] Not because of any normative pre-eminence over other normative bodies that would naturally elect the state as the entity holding sway over the others, but because the state legal order could rely on an incomparably larger amount of legal expertise.[14] At the same time, this expertise, as a special kind of knowledge, came with a special obligation, that is, to pave the way for a negotiation between the state and substate groups within the bounds of the existing constitutional order. Still, this was not meant to assimilate substate groups into the state legal order, but to feed the latter with new energies for a new (legal) vision of the social and its complexity.

In Romano's view, therefore, the solution to those years of struggle was the establishment of a novel and more flexible constitution comprising norms that could gradually evolve with a view to accommodating social reality and its continuous changes. These norms can arise out of the interaction of nonstate orders and the state order, as the latter tries to accommodate the normativity of the former. A constitutional order that should not have any aspiration to completeness, but rather should deliberately pursue incompleteness to prevent the fossilization of extant legal forms and categories.[15] All in all, he reasoned, the state should survive and be amended exactly because it was the only agency that possessed the tools to accomplish this end. No special attachment to the historical political form that the state was. Only the unswerving conviction that a complex but open-textured conception of the social calls for refined

12 It might be argued that the other long-lived institution that Romano thought to possess such a notable pool of legal resources is the Church, particularly, the Catholic Church.
13 See L. Vinx, 'Santi Romano against the State?' (2018) 2 *Ethics & Global Politics* 25–36. It is worth stressing that, unlike the author of the present introduction, Vinx puts emphasis on the tensions that he believes exist between legal institutionalism, with its normative assumptions, and Romano's commitments to legal positivism and legal pluralism.
14 It should be noted that this does not exclude that legal expertise is also maintained and developed outside the state. Romano's claim is certainly not that the state has the monopoly on the legal, but that the state creates the appropriate conditions for developing and nurturing massive amount of legal knowledge.
15 Romano's idea is not to deliberately pursue incompleteness, but rather to achieve completeness by using flexible and open norms. In this context, the different roles of legislators and judges should be emphasized: legislators should limit themselves to enacting general laws, while leaving to judges the interpretation and further development of these laws in particular social areas.

Santi Romano before legal institutionalism 11

legal doctrine and a class of experts who cultivate it. As we will see in the following sections, this is but the flip side of Romano's conception of necessity.

A preliminary matter of fair comparison: Does necessity look like Schmitt's exception?

Before I delve into this topic, it is important to make a point to eschew any potential metaunderstandings. For 'On the Decree-laws' is still regarded by some scholars as the anticipation of a stream of thought that would become central in the conceptualization of state authority – one that locates this authority in the ability to declare and use emergencies as a formidable governmental technique. Notoriously, this is the received view of the political theorizing of Carl Schmitt, who is alleged to be the doyen of exceptionalist theorists as well as the staunchest advocate of the state monopoly on the political semantics of what counts as an emergency. In the light of these concerns, most scholars have long interpreted Schmitt as the holder of the view that the state of exception is the uttermost manifestation of political authority, the one that defines who the holder of sovereignty is – and this explains why the state, on his view, should never allow other entities to establish what counts as an emergency and what the population should understand and fight as such.[16] Although

16 This is the interpretation that Andrea Salvatore and I examine and rebut in M. Croce and A. Salvatore, *Carl Schmitt's Institutional Theory*, op. cit. fn. 10. We certainly do not turn a blind eye to Schmitt's fixation for the exception in the early 1920s but draw attention to what came ahead and after that transitory phase. The main claim we make is that Schmitt's most robust and pondered theory is the substantive, ultra-conservative legal institutionalism that he developed from the late 1920s till the 1950s, one that is utterly incompatible with Schmitt's exceptionalist intimations in *Political Theology* (1922). Amongst the works that move away from the exceptionalist interpretation and put stress on Schmitt's works after 1927 are D. Bates, 'Political Theology and the Nazi State: Carl Schmitt's Concept of the Institution' (2006) 3 *Modern Intellectual History* 415–442; H. Lindahl, 'Law as Concrete Order. Schmitt and the Problem of Collective Freedom' in *Law, Liberty and State: Oakeshott, Hayek, and Schmitt on the Rule of Law*, eds. David Dyzenhaus and Thomas Poole (Cambridge: Cambridge University Press, 2017), pp. 38–64; M. Loughlin, *Politonomy*, in J. Meierhenrich and O. Simons (eds), *The Oxford Handbook of Carl Schmitt* (Oxford: Oxford University Press, 2016); J. Meierhenrich, 'Fearing the Disorder of Things: The Development of Carl Schmitt's Institutional Theory. 1919–1942' in Meierhenrich and Simons (eds), *The Oxford Handbook of Carl Schmitt*, pp. 171–216.

12 *Santi Romano before legal institutionalism*

this interpretation of Schmitt's thinking has largely been dethroned for quite some time now, it certainly captures an important phase in his lengthy scholarly career. This is the one running from 1921 to 1927, when he did toy with the idea that the state of exception should be treated as the major concept in the toolkit of legal and political theory. So, while Schmitt after that period mostly got rid of the notion of exception and substantially scaled down the power of state authorities to use and misuse emergencies, in the present context it comes as an intellectual duty to consider his exceptionalist phase to delineate and make out a view that *should by no means be attributed* to Romano.[17]

As the issue of the exception in Schmitt's theory has duly deserved a voluminous literature, in this section I will mainly look at those elements of it that are relevant to pinpointing Romano's position on the matter. Schmitt's main insight in *Political Theology* (1922)[18] was that the exception is a *de facto* situation whose occurrence and nature cannot be predicted, and hence cannot be regulated by any positive law. By saying 'de facto,' I obviously do not mean 'factual,' 'a matter of fact,' because, as I will point out shortly, it is considered by Schmitt as the fountainhead of law. It is only with respect to a positive constitution that an exception is *de facto*, in the sense that it exceeds its scope and escapes the normative claim of its norms. The exception, in his view, is that which cannot be included into the positive legal order – a situation that no positive legal norms can say what to do about and how. More concretely, Schmitt thought that Art. 48 of the Weimar constitution, which defined and tried to regulate the state of exception (*Ausnahmezustand*), was wanting, to say the least. It allowed the President of the Reich to suppress, momentarily, a few key fundamental rights to cope with extreme crises menacing the order to restore the latter. But the constitutional text was neither clear nor complete. He was of the opinion that the limits to the President's activities were specified so loosely that Art. 48 could even be used to install a new order – and should that happen, the state of exception could certainly not be interpreted as an instrument to protect the constitution. For it

---

17 The relation between Romano's and Schmitt's theories is more complicated than I can elucidate in this text. Two articles that deftly delve into it are M. de Wilde, 'The Dark Side of Institutionalism: Carl Schmitt Reading Santi Romano' (2018) 11(2) *Ethics & Global Politics* 12–24, and A. Salvatore, 'A Counter-Mine that Explodes Silently: Romano and Schmitt on the Unity of the Legal Order' (2018) 11(2) *Ethics & Global Politics* 50–59.

18 C. Schmitt, *Political Theology: Four Chapters on the Concept of Sovereignty* (Chicago: University of Chicago Press, 2005).

Santi Romano before legal institutionalism 13

was an instrument to abolish the existing constitutional order and to bring about something entirely new.[19]

Surely enough, this was no reason for Schmitt to expunge the exception from the realm of legal theorizing. Quite the opposite, he thought it is precisely in such a non-includible circumstance that one should find the answer to the key question of what the legal order is and how it is brought about. Despite the titillating reference to the miracle,[20] there is nothing truly miraculous in the genesis of a legal order. Schmitt's reasoning is straightforward, even naïve, one could say. He held the view that a legal order subsists insofar as the normality underpinning it continues to subsist – where 'normality' stands for the consolidated, ordinary ways people regularly carry out the various practices comprising their daily life. The legal order can only regulate an already ordered social context. But when this normality gets disrupted, there is little the legal order can do. It just goes on the blink. And here comes Schmitt's characterizing feature in his exceptionalist phase: he maintains that the normality of a social context is really suspended only when the sovereign *decides* it is. In other words, the sovereign is one who takes it upon himself to declare that the situation is abnormal, that the laws that are meant to govern ordinary practices are inapplicable, and that therefore the whole legal order is to be suspended. If one succeeds in this (whether this one is the President or any other individual), one *turns oneself* into the sovereign.

19 It is worth emphasizing that, in Schmitt's view, the most serious danger was that the sovereign would be unable to protect the existing constitution should he remain strictly bound to positive legal norms (as liberals and legal positivists such as Hugo Preuss and Richard Grau suggested). A superb analysis of this topic is M. De Wilde, 'The State of Emergency in the Weimar Republic Legal Disputes over Article 48 of the Weimar Constitution' (2010) 78(1–2) *The Legal History Review* 135–158. See also W. Scheuerman, 'States of Emergency,' in *The Oxford Handbook of Carl Schmitt*, eds. J. Meierhenrich and O. Simons (Oxford: Oxford University Press, 2016), pp. 547–469, and J. McCormick, 'Identifying or Exploiting the Paradoxes of Constitutional Democracy? An Introduction to Carl Schmitt's *Legality and Legitimacy*,' in C. Schmitt, *Legality and Legitimacy*, trans. and edited by Jeffrey Seitzer, with an Introduction by John P. McCormick (Durham and London: Duke University Press, 2004), pp. xiii–xliii.

20 'The exception in jurisprudence is analogous to the miracle in theology' (Schmitt, *Political Theology*, 36). This however should not lead astray. For the miracle is intended to represent an action that is not comprised within the chain of causes and effects governed by physical laws – just like the sovereign's creation of the order is not authorized and regulated by any pre-existing law.

14 *Santi Romano before legal institutionalism*

In a sense that will prove crucial in the next pages, in the exception Schmitt did not so much see a problem of efficacy as *an exercise in socio-political semantics.* The Schmittian sovereign is one who does not simply attest to the fact that the laws are inapplicable and that more stringent measures are needed. Much more than this, the sovereign is the one who engenders a phase change – he determines that the crisis is not a mere emergency and that it calls for utterly new socio-political coordinates. This means that the sovereign incarnates the order, as it were; his activities initiate the order, which develops *as a consequence of* her archetypal deed; the new order could not exist without the sovereign's decision that a new order is called for.[21] This is a crucial difference with Romano's notion of necessity, which not by chance cannot be easily qualified as either an emergency or an exception. Granted: necessity, as we will have to see, is the origin of law. But Romano's picture does not involve any decisionism, let alone any demiurge.

Necessity as law

As I insisted above, Romano's break with the state-centred tradition in legal scholarship was remarkable. He did not consider the state as the producer of the law, and thereby escaped the dilemma of what it is that limits the agency which is authorized to set the limits. At the same time, contrary to Georg Jellinek's influential position, he rejected the view that the state's origins are purely factual. There is no (juristically) accountable passage from the factual to the legal. If we combine these two assumptions, in Romano's view, the state cannot originate from an act of will that transforms a matter of fact into a legal reality. Early in

---

21 An element that deserves mention here is that Schmitt's position in *Political Theology* is radical and extreme. The sovereign *creates* the order, and thus his suspension of the preceding order is conducive to a new order. In other, more technical works devoted to Art. 48, his position is less radical, as it was meant to demonstrate that the existing order could only be safeguarded if the President was granted more extensive emergency powers: in other words, protecting the existing order (i.e., the fundamental political decision underlying the existing constitution) required a more extensive authority to derogate from positive constitutional norms. Moreover, Schmitt's position evolved over time to the extent that in the early 1930s he ceased to trust in the salvific power of the President. For example, Schmitt's *Legality and Legitimacy* (Durham, NC: Duke University Press), published in 1932, put forward quite a different strategy to save the Weimar constitution, one that was not pivoted on the President's powers, but on an institutionalist, ultraconservative conception of the constitutional state.

the first decade of the 20th century, Romano devoted two essays to these questions: *L'instaurazione di fatto di un ordinamento costituzionale e sua legittimazione* (The *de facto* establishment of a constitutional order and its legitimation), published in 1901, and *Osservazioni preliminari per una teoria sui limiti della funzione legislativa nel diritto italiano* (Preliminary remarks for a theory on the limits of the legislative function in Italian law), published in 1902.

Romano certainly did not think that a law which is superior to positive law is there to set limits to the state's authority. In that respect, he was an unrepented positivist: law and conventional morality can and do intersect in many ways, but they amount to different orders. Put otherwise, law and morality are two distinct normative practices that often overlap because of the conducts they claim to govern and the agents they address. If it is true that morality claims a special pre-eminence by which the law is supposed to conform to moral norms, this conformity is conceptually indifferent to the law. Romano saw no reason why immoral law – or better, a law that is deemed as immoral according to the standards of the morality in question – should not be considered as law. This is why there is not, and there cannot be (conceptually in the first place), a law of nature that restrains positive and statutory law. Rather, Romano argues, what limits the legislative function is the positive constitution itself, for it rigidly bounds the competences it grants the legislature. However, in both essays, he insists that the legislator can or even should flex constitutional boundaries when *necessity* arises. Interestingly, he addresses such a particular condition as necessity as one in which the legislator 'does not invent, but collects and declares the law it discovers in the general consciousness, so to say, coercively, which excludes its intellectual and personal mediation.'[22]

What deserves attention here is that the legislative power is tasked with carrying out not a creative process but an *act of recognition*. Necessity brings to the surface a law that the legislature is called upon to recognize, even against the constitution if the appropriate circumstances arise. The legislator derives this special power to cross constitutional barriers because *necessity as the primary source of law commands it* (more than simply authorize). By doing so, necessity prompts, so to say, the legislator to make sure that the constitution remains constantly flexible and porous. Italian legal historian Maurizio Fioravanti nicely captures such a key role of necessity. He points out

---

22 S. Romano, 'Osservazioni preliminari per una teoria sui limiti della funzione legislativa nel diritto italiano,' in S. Romano, *Lo Stato moderno e la sua crisi* (Milano: Giuffrè, 1969), pp. 119–150, 143.

16 Santi Romano before legal institutionalism

that for Romano the virtue of a flexible constitution is that it sets limits and at the same time allows continuous amendments. The linchpin of this virtuous dynamics is necessity as that which unveils the law that awaits recognition – therefore, neither a closed-off document nor the power of a state agency. It is by dint of the notion of necessity that Romano, 'on the one hand, does not fall back on natural law, and on the other hand, pursues his ideal of a legally limited state. ... The law of "necessity" is the only one that can perform this function, because it is the only extra-state type of law that does not bring into play the sovereign centrality of the modern state.'[23]

In what follows, I will try to elucidate what this limitation amounts to. Basically, while necessity justifies derogation from constitutional norms, Romano is certainly aware of the risk that the state may use necessity as a pretext to ignore constitutional barriers and to tighten its clutch on society. However, he believes necessity is itself a source of law – superior to positive law – that entails limitations to state power: the state's response must be sensitive to the requirements of necessity, and these, in their turn, bring to light social needs and pressures, which the state cannot ignore. In addition, at the end of 'On the Decree-laws,' Romano insists that the state is required to conform to the legal provisions that set the temporal frame of the state of siege and to act in such a way as to overcome the crisis. But these are not the main reasons why he thinks that necessity limits, and not increases, the power of the state. To penetrate his reasoning, we need to unpack the notion of necessity in the first place. At this stage I should like to recall that, for him, there is no passage from the fact to the law that explains the birth of the state normative order. If that is the case, normativity is somewhat a primordial phenomenon: it comes ahead of the factual, so much as that, as far as legality is concerned, a purely factual state of affairs is a nonsense. I would now like to illustrate this by briefly introducing Romano's reasoning.

On 28 December 1908, early in the morning an earthquake with a moment magnitude of 7.1 and a maximum Mercalli intensity of XI struck the cities of Messina and Reggio Calabria. With epicentre in the municipality of Reggio Calabria, the earthquake is considered one of the most powerful and devastating earthquakes in Italian history. Beside destroying entire buildings, the Calabrian-Sicilian earthquake interrupted all communication routes (roads, railways, tramways, telegraph, and telephone). Half of the population of Messina and one-third of the population of the Calabrian city died. Messina's entire

23 Fioravanti, *La scienza del diritto pubblico*, 317.

Santi Romano before legal institutionalism   17

historic centre was devastated. On 2 January 1909, a state of siege was proclaimed by the King, and full powers were given to General Francesco Mazza for maintaining public order and security.[24] This is the exceptional, unexpected context that Romano found himself commenting on.

He clarifies why the situation is unusual and requires urgent action: if the state of siege as a measure to respond to a natural disaster was nothing Italian law provided for, based on what did the government declare it? Was it a legal, an a-legal, or extra-legal action? In Italy, the Statuto Albertino did not provide for any reduction or limitation of the constitutional guarantees.[25] However, the state of siege was considered legitimate based on the King's power to declare war and command the army. In the wake of the earthquake, legal scholars engaged in a heated debate on the legal grounds of the state of siege extended to natural calamities. A key figure in public law at the time, Oreste Ranelletti (1868–1956), first brought up the issue of necessity, which he thought allowed the state to limit the citizens' rights and freedoms in an unprecedented way, especially as far as the imposed general exodus was concerned. A new conception of subjective public rights was emerging, he reasoned, whereby the state was expanding its powers through emergency measures. Ranelletti called attention to the law of 17 July 1898, no. 297, establishing that the King's government could in case of necessity declare a state of siege and, in general, issue emergency decrees subject to the approval of parliament. On this account, the state of siege fell under the scope of criminal law, thus within a specific branch of state law, which authorized the government's activity. At the opposite extreme of this debate, constitutional lawyer Ettore Lombardo Pellegrino (1866–1952) argued that the state of siege was a *de facto* measure that fell outside the scope of the constitution. It was understandable and justifiable, given the risks the earthquake posed, but it fundamentally remained *contra legem*. The justification of the administrative action

24 For a nice description of the events and the aftermath, see Massimo La Torre, 'La fine dell'Ottocento. Il terremoto di Messina e lo stato d'eccezione' (2009) 1 *Materiali per una storia della cultura giuridica* 97–124.
25 The Statuto Albertino (4 March 1848) was the constitution granted to his subjects by King Charles Albert of Piedmont-Sardinia. It later became the constitution of the Kingdom of Italy when Italy was unified under Piedmontese leadership in 1861. Originally very conservative, it was subsequently amended to fit with the liberal parliamentary government of the late 19th and early 20th centuries. The Statuto remained the grounds of the Italian legal order through to the fascist regime, though it suffered deep modifications. It lasted until the implementation of the republican constitution in 1948.

18 *Santi Romano before legal institutionalism*

should occur *ex post facto*, based on the idea of a flexible constitution that was able to include originally a-legal or even anti-legal measures.

These were amongst the most influential positions that Romano criticizes and rejects in 'On the Decree-laws.' Certainly, he seized on the idea of necessity being the key element in the picture, but he gave it a crucial, foundational role, well beyond that of a justificatory basis for new bodies of state law. His provoking statement is that necessity is 'the first and original source of all law, so much so that, with respect to it, the other sources are somewhat to be considered as derived.'[26] But if this is the case, it is obviously true that Romano was not thinking of necessity as a bare fact, an unexpected mishap requiring special attention from the government.[27] Much more than this, according to him, it is 'a given state of affairs ... that constitutes an explicit, urgent, and categorical manifestation of needs and social forces.'[28] In short, if necessity does possess a factual element, what makes it so special in the life of the law is that it is a *normative fact* with a *nomic force*. For it has the extraordinary potential of yielding normativity. Necessity 'immediately and directly' releases 'a compulsory norm,' 'with no uncertainty and no possibility of getting away with it.'[29] In a word, necessity *is* law.

I can now return to the recognition process that the legislator is called on to perform. Necessity bears an *unstated* nomic power that needs verbalizing. The legislature's job is to distillate the normative standards and principles that necessity sets forth so violently and blindly. In this sense, hardly can necessity fall within the scope of the existing constitution, as it is the manifestation of something that is not originally included and demands inclusion. But there is no facile relation of inside/outside with the order that is being challenged. The

---

26 Supra, 36.
27 Romano does not elaborate on a conception that would have supported his argument, that is, the traditional distinction between necessity as a bare fact and necessity as a legal norm. For example, in late medieval legal thought, the principle 'necessity has no law' did not refer to an extra-juridical necessity, that is, a purely *de facto* situation outside the sphere of law. Instead, it was developed as a legal concept; a legal judgment was necessary only in so far as it was legally judged to be so. For instance, Gratian and Aquinas tended to qualify *necessitas* in legal terms. Not every necessity was recognized as *necessitas* in the legal sense, but only 'supreme,' 'pressing,' 'urgent,' and 'evident' necessity. On this tradition, see M. de Wilde, 'Emergency Powers and Constitutional Change in the Late Middle Ages' (2015) 83(1–2) *Tijdschrift voor Rechtsgeschiedenis/Legal History Review*, 26–59, at 35–36.
28 Supra, 36.
29 Supra, 36.

Santi Romano before legal institutionalism 19

relation is intrinsic: necessity is by no means an alien order that merely menaces taking over the existing one, but is a law that appeals to the existing order in that 'it is aimed at defending the order from a hostile force, or at restoring its effectiveness, if this, for whatever reason, even involuntary, has ceased to exist, and is moreover felt and translated into contingent rules by the constituted powers.'[30] At the same time, it is naturally *contra legem* in that the constitution does not regulate it. In short, it is an a-legal or even illegal nomic power that brings into light the limits of the existing positive law. Or better, as I will insist, necessity is an unwritten law that is illegal in the eyes of the state order and asks for an immediate amendment of positive law.

Romano's insight is considerable: necessity does not lie in the realm of the factual but in that of the normative. It owns an unverbalized nomic force awaiting verbalization. It is non-legal only in the sense that positive law does not encompass it, but it is legal through and through because it claims authority over the existing constitution. His conclusion is that the state of siege 'is a measure contrary to the law, let us say illegal, but at the same time conforming to positive unwritten law, and therefore legal and constitutional, seems to be most correct and convenient.'[31] This is also why, Romano concludes, the activities called for by necessity are to conform to the requirements of the existing legal order, and the government is mandated to conform to what the constitution imposes. This is a conspicuously different conception than Schmitt's exception as the peak of political power.[32] The voluntary element of a sovereign declaring the end of ordinary life vanishes to the extent that the legislator or the government is deemed to be someone who recognizes – hardly wills or imposes. In addition, necessity can be addressed with emergency decrees only when the law proves inapplicable

---

30 Supra, 37.
31 Supra, 37.
32 It should be noted that Schmitt himself in *Constitutional Theory* (Durham, NC: Duke University Press, 2008) would probably say that it all comes down to what one means by 'constitution.' If one refers to the constitution as a 'complete decision over the type and form of the political unity' (75), then he would argue that the sovereign is mandated to conform to what the constitution imposes. However, if one refers to the constitution as a 'multitude of individual laws' (67), then he would argue that the sovereign is not mandated to conform, as he is allowed to derogate from the constitution. My interpretative take, however, is that *Constitutional Theory* represents a turning point in Schmitt's thinking, one that would be conducive to his institutional conception of law of the early 1930s. So, in this introduction I am mainly referring to Schmitt's theorization of the state of exception and the power of the sovereign in the early 1920s.

20 *Santi Romano before legal institutionalism*

and state law ceases to function. But this is nothing political agencies can establish on their own. Rather, their duty is to understand the needs and forces that necessity calls attention to. Authorities must be wise and perceptive, not self-founding and demiurgic.

On the road to legal institutionalism

In this final section, however, I would like to spell out the relation of the two essays translated in this book to the magnum opus, *The Legal Order*. In 1909, Romano could not still count on a fully-fledged theoretical toolkit to make sense of what he was seeking to conceptualize. Put otherwise, he lacked the notion of institution as the core nature of the legal phenomenon, which would be the gist of *The Legal Order*. It is not for this introduction to summarize his seminal theory,[33] but it is worth recalling that the institution is an organizational process that takes place in every sphere of the social. I should correct myself, though, as the institution *is* the social, because all that is social is organized. Anytime a practice surpasses the contingency of the moment and sets standards for them to be repeated in the future, this is the spark of the social. And this is also the quintessence of the legal, according to Romano. The institution comprises the various set of techniques that the members of a practice employ to allow their practice to perdure. In this sense, the constitutive elements of an institution are at least two: the techniques that are meant to ensure compliance and repetition (norms of various nature, pressure, rituals, theoretical principles – certainly not only legal rules or official coercion) and the knowledge that is meant to reflect

---

33 The Anglophone literature on *The Legal Order* is happily expanding. Among the most recent works that help unpack its main themes, see F. Fontanelli, 'Santi Romano and *L'ordinamento giuridico*: The Relevance of a Forgotten Masterpiece for Contemporary International, Transnational and Global Legal Relations' (2011) 2(1) *Transnational Legal Theory* 67–117; M. Loughlin, *Political Jurisprudence* (Oxford: Oxford University Press, 2017), especially Chap. 6; Giulio Itzcovich '"Something More Lively and Animated Than the Law": Institutionalism and Formalism in Santi Romano's Jurisprudence' (2020) 33(2) *Ratio Juris* 241–257; M. La Torre, 'Institutionalism as Alternative Constitutional Theory: On Santi Romano's Concept of Law and his Epigones' (2020) 11(1) *Jurisprudence* 92–100; C. Mac Amhlaigh 'Constitutional pluralism Avant la Lettre?: on Santi Romano's *L'ordinamento giuridico*' (2020) 11(1) *Jurisprudence* 101–113; S. I. Tschorne 'What is in a word? *The Legal Order* and the Turn from "Norms" to "Institutions" in Legal Thought' (2020) 11(1) *Jurisprudence* 114–130; F. Fontanelli, 'Review of Santi Romano. *The Legal Order*' (2021) 31(4) *European Journal of International Law* 1537–1544.

Santi Romano before legal institutionalism 21

on how they should be used and regulated. With words that are not Romano's, *techniques plus technology*. But if that is the case, the institution (i.e., the law) is something that inheres in every human practice that aspires to be repeatable. State law is nothing other than a specialized, time-tested, highly complex institution among others that might be simpler but no less legal.

In my view, as early as 1901 Romano had the insight that the social, if it is social, is always and already organized. There is no pre-legal moment or phase that is only social – all organized patterns of behaviour are legal insofar as they are organized. This means that, even when a calamity occurs, if social interaction continues and new ways of coping with the dramatic situation emerge, there is a law that is taking shape. If this law is different than the law that governed social life before the calamity came about, a conflict of laws is likely to arise. The state legal order is being replaced not by chaos but by an embryonic legal order. State authorities, then, are required to undertake a process of recognition whereby state law strives to include the new legal order within its provisions. We could describe this as a negotiation between orders: one that is being challenged and one that is making inroads. Romano's words are crystal clear: for necessity

> to remain within the realm of positive law … it is sufficient that it manifests itself as a force that defends and protects the existing order and is translated into commands of the state. If it manifests itself in the opposite sense, there is no denying that real law can arise from it. However, this will happen at a later stage, if and when it succeeds in constituting the power and the regime that will take it from the state of abstract justice to that of the state of concrete and stable order. Necessity can therefore give rise to legal measures, even when these are contrary to the law.[34]

Romano has no doubts that necessity is law – since it is the production context of organized behaviour – and that one cannot predict how this dynamic will evolve. The state's response to necessity is a recognition process that prevents the establishment of a law that is contrary to its own norms and principles. But this theorization makes complete sense in the light of the institutional theory that he would soon put forward. All instances of organized behaviour are a combination of techniques and knowledge about techniques that can instantiate long-term patterns of regulated behaviour. Certainly, in both essays, Romano roots for the state. But there is no contradiction with the steadfast defence of

34 Supra, 38.

22 Santi Romano before legal institutionalism

the institutional pluralism to come. For he thinks that the state, although it is an institution among institutions, counts on a repertoire of techniques and technology that is incomparably larger and more sophisticated along with a class of trained experts who master them with unmatchable proficiency. If the law is to be a venue for negotiation, the outcome of the latter depends on the degree of professionality and the quality of the expertise. This explains the famous metaphor of state law as a field that lends itself to ever-new construction:

> For in this way the struggle that nowadays seems to be directed against [modern constitutions] is likely to take on a different character if people realize that it is occurring in a field where there are no trenches to dismantle, but only defences to raise. To build and not to destroy: this is, more than anything else, the task that can and must be set, with respect to the political order, the evolution of our social life; and, once the new edifice has been built, it probably will no longer be at variance with the solid and severe architecture of the modern state, but will rest on its very foundations and will constitute integral part of it.[35]

This is a conservative reformist speaking – one who firmly believes that the law is the supreme governmental technique and that the jurists should be those who oversee its employment. And probably this is his major limit: the idea that the law has a natural proclivity for ensuring social peace and cooperation and that all that is touched by juristic knowledge is destined to be recomposed within a conciliatory frame. This is certainly the jurist's irenicism that makes him blind to the exclusionary potential of law. But this introduction is not the place to assess Romano's project as a whole. All that I aimed to do was to shine a light on the unquestionable value of the essays that appear in this book and their relation to one of the most important theories in 20th-century legal theory. In this regard, it was important to understand why and how Romano thought the state should be preserved – and his hunch was that preservation meant thoroughgoing restructuring. History went down a different road and Romano did contribute to this wicked path when he was the President of the Council of State from 15 December 1928 to 11 October 1944.[36] This, however, does not

---

35 Supra, 61–62.
36 On Romano's conduct as the President of the Council of State, see A. Romano *et al.*, *La giustizia amministrativa ai tempi di Santi Romano presidente del Consiglio di Stato* (Torino: Giappichelli, 2004).

diminish the significance of a theory that does speak to us today, when saving the existing constitutions implies rethinking their role and structures well beyond the legacy of WWII.

Acknowledgements

I'm heavily indebted to Marc de Wilde, Marco Goldoni, and Andrea Salvatore for their meticulous reading of this text. In particular, a few formulations of specific junctures are due to Marc's acute comments on some key points that were unclear and wanting in a former draft. Responsibility for all faults and omissions remains mine alone.

1 On the Decree Laws and the State of Siege During the Earthquakes in Messina and Reggio Calabria[1]

Some of the measures taken by the government after the Calabrian-Sicilian earthquake – before the law of 12 January, especially Art. 6 and 14, conferred on it extraordinary powers – deserve meticulous attention. For they gave a new and characteristic shape to a power that the government has always abundantly employed, as is well known, but in very different circumstances and for very different purposes. The power in question is that of issuing urgent decree laws and of establishing the so-called civil state of siege. This latter power should be discussed separately, because, quite rightly, the view that it is a mere, particular manifestation of the former is not generally agreed-upon.

Everybody knows that in such a delicate matter, which touches on the supreme principles and the foundations of our constitutional order, there is no certainty – both in the theory, which has devoted to it numerous and sometimes valuable studies, and in the practice, despite the many and frequent circumstances in which it has materialized so far. Naturally, the most considerable uncertainties and, one might say, the most frustrating ones, are to be found in the doctrine. On this subject-matter, the doctrine has carried out its critical task in such a way that even simply expressing one's view proves far from easy. Views go from the one that simplistically denies the government having the powers in question, to others that, on very different grounds, recognize their legitimacy or, at least, justify their *de facto* exercise in the most different degrees and with the most disparate consequences and conditions.[2] It goes without saying that many of these uncertainties had an immediate impact on the practice – not so much on the government's

---

1   See Longhi 1909.
2   For a reliable account of the various perspectives on the state of siege, see Ranelletti 1904; and finally, on top of the state of siege, also on the various forms of emergency decrees, see the interesting study Gmelin 1907.

DOI: 10.4324/9781003347774-2

practice as on both the judicial and the parliamentary one, which often and for various reasons have even increased and intensified these uncertainties. The aim of this writing – it is worth noting – cannot be a rehearsal of the whole theory. Rather, it intends to draw the attention of scholars to some of its points that the recent case illuminated in an unforeseen and, perhaps, unforeseeable way. One of the reasons why the theory is affected by many flaws is that it has been formulated always on the occasion of, and with regard to, cases that actually occurred, while these have always shown the same, familiar characteristics. Therefore, the doctrine, or rather the various doctrines that have been produced could not purge themselves of some degree of unilateralism, which prevented them from arriving at more general principles despite all the efforts of acute minds. It should be added that the 'precedents' to which I referred, because of their very nature, were not impermeable to various and extreme political considerations, which, albeit inadvertently, can sometimes affect and inspire the most expert and dispassionate jurist. On the contrary, while, as I observed, the measures that I will home in on here concern a case that is very different from the usual ones, they lie in a field that is most removed from the concerns and prejudices of everyday politics.

The first of such measures, because of its importance, is the Royal Decree of 3 January. which reads as follows:

> Having regard to Art. 243 of the Penal Code for the Army; considering that the cataclysmic earthquake of December 28, 1908, in the territories of Messina and Reggio Calabria have created a situation that is in some respects identical to, and in others more serious than, that occurring in territories that are in a state of war; having regard to the need and urgent necessity to provide immediately for all the public services which have ceased to exist, and for public order and safety; given that the ordinary jurisdiction has ceased to exist and that it is impossible to re-establish it immediately; on the proposal of the Council of Ministers,

a state of siege is declared in the municipality of Messina[3] and in the municipalities of the district of Reggio.

Apart from the case of war, the state of siege has so far been proclaimed as a police measure: the energetic and swift protection of public order on the occasion of those popular uprisings which are

---

3 By Royal Decree of 8 January, the state of siege was then extended to the district of Messina.

26   *On the Decree Laws*

named in various ways according to their seriousness, from a simple riot to the extreme case of a revolution. More than that, this objective and this characteristic were deemed to be so essential and indispensable that the doctrine integrated them into the notion itself of the state of siege. All the definitions of the state of siege, without exception – which makes any quotation superfluous – are based on the assumption of an attack against the constitutional order in force, of an uprising against public powers, of a criminal disorder brought about by internal enemies of the state. The question has been raised as to whether the state of siege should only serve to repress such movements, or whether it can also have a purely preventive purpose; but in any case, no one had so far thought that it could find its *raison d'être* in causes other than those. And it is easy to understand to what extent this has affected the whole theoretical formulation of the thorny problems that are connected to this issue. At present, these problems are to be formulated and resolved in such a way as to include the case, like the present one, of a state of siege imposed not in order to tackle an unlawful collective activity against the existing order, but to remedy the dissolution of every social and political organization that has occurred due to a completely involuntary and natural phenomenon. On this account, there is no struggle against rebels to protect the law, while the repression of common crimes perpetrated by those who incline to take advantage of the favourable opportunity for their criminal agenda represents an utterly secondary aim, however important it may be. The principal aim, well before any further needs, is to restore public services, which turn out to be more vital than in ordinary times, both because of the effects of the cataclysm that public services must cope with and because of the difficulty in replacing them with the private initiative. And in addition to administrative needs, attention should be paid to those relating to the judicial function, which remained paralyzed and suspended. The motivation for the decree of 3 January has briefly but incisively highlighted these causes, which determined the measure established with it. This confers on this measure interesting and original characteristics.

Let me begin with the scrutiny of the decree itself to see what doctrinal consequences can be drawn from it. It is worth noting that, like the previous ones on the subject of the state of siege, this decree was considered to be based on the well-known provisions of the penal code for the army, which regulate the state of war. It is not easy to determine how this was done in the past; but amongst the various interpretations that I evoked above, I think one can be definitely ruled out in this new case. I mean the view that the civil state of siege falls within the scope of the state of war and should therefore be regulated by the military penal code, so much so that the power of the government to proclaim it is claimed to rest on a direct and express legal provision. In truth, this view did not meet with success, but it was stated that this is precisely the one that has been adopted by the Italian practice in several declarations of the state of siege.[4] However, without a doubt, this does not apply to the latest decree. To some extent and with a lot of good will, one could make sense of the identification of the two figures – though the dominant doctrine has always rightly rejected it – and consider a simple internal revolt as a war. Yet, no one could reasonably hold that the military penal code contemplates the state of affairs that was engendered by the earthquake in Messina and Reggio. Indeed, the decree of 3 January felt the need to point out the difference between the two cases, though at the same time it emphasized the similarities. For it observed that the situation brought about by the cataclysm was *in some respects identical* and *in others more serious* than that which occurs in territories that are in a state of war. Therefore, one cannot help but recognize that the reference to the aforesaid provisions was not due to the fact that it [the present state of siege] is covered by them, but to *extend* these provisions to a case which they do not regulate. This inevitably begs the question: What are the grounds for this extension?

It is well known that the doctrine has always held, with considerable emphasis, that it is impossible to elicit these grounds from an analogical interpretation. There is no denying that the figure of the state of siege is akin to that of the state of war, especially if one has in mind, as has been done so far, the circumstance of a state of siege caused by a revolt. No matter how numerous and serious the differences are between a revolt and a war in the true sense of the word, it would nevertheless be paradoxical to deny the blatant similarities.[5] Such similarities, in my opinion, although attenuated, still subsist even in the case of a state of siege akin to that to which the territories of Messina and Reggio were subjected – and it was actually not without reason that they were alluded to and emphasized, in the grounds for the Royal decree, in the words to which I referred above. Moreover, the fact itself of the possibility, or even the necessity, of applying the so-called martial law in those conditions stands out as a practical but conclusive argument that the case in question is, from certain points of view and for certain effects, similar to that expressly contemplated by the very

4   Ranelletti 1904, 1166, fn. 1.
5   Against this view, however, see Racioppi 1909.

28 *On the Decree Laws*

same law. However, some have advanced a more robust argument. Given that the rules relating to the state of war are utterly exceptional and restrictive of individual freedom, far from being applicable on the basis of sheer analogy, they cannot even be extensively interpreted in the same relationships to which they refer.[6] Here I need not explore the true meaning of Art. 4 of the preliminary provisions of the Civil Code, which enshrines this principle of hermeneutics in which some people seem to have blind faith. The idea that an exceptional provision cannot be extended to cover cases that fall within the rule against which the exception arises is obvious, more than right. For it follows from the easy observation that the exception would otherwise no longer be an exception and the rule would no longer be a rule. But the idea that an exceptional norm cannot be extended to cover a case different from the one to which it refers, but just as exceptional – and therefore not covered by the rule – as well as analogous, maybe needs justifying. However, since I believe that the problem must be located on a different ground, it is no use insisting on this point. But I cannot help pointing out the contradiction in which, I think, one falls into when one puts the question in these terms – and this demonstrates the logical impossibility of adhering to these terms.

For some scholars aver that the grounds for extending the military penal code to the case of a state of siege is not to be found in analogy, but rather in the state's necessity to provide for such an extension.[7] And by necessity, as we will see more clearly in a moment, they do not mean something that immediately generates a norm, a legal precept, which is itself a *source of* law. Rather, they mean a condition, a state of things to which the law [diritto obbiettivo] that implicitly or explicitly arises from the *laws* [leggi], from our written law [diritto scritto], is claimed to attribute certain effects. But I fail to understand how necessity, so conceived, instead of analogy, and despite the juridical impossibility of the latter, can furnish a legitimate reason for extending a rule to a case that it does not cover. I believe it would be more correct to say that precisely this state of necessity, which is presupposed by

6 Thus, among many others, Cammeo 1898, 14; Racioppi, 1909, 280; Ranelletti 1904, 1202.
7 The argument of necessity is rightly used by all those who admit the legitimacy of the state of siege, but often in terms that are technically very indefinite. Therefore, it is impossible to determine with certainty whether the criticism of the text also refers to them, although it likely does. Formulated with great precision and in such a way as to remove all doubts, in the sense that I believe should be disproved, is the opinion by Ranelletti 1904, 1202 ff.

On the Decree Laws 29

the rule itself as well as by the state of siege to which it is intended to apply, is what contributes to establishing the analogy between the two cases, so much so that ultimately it is analogy that provides the grounds for the extension. If one does not want to come to this conclusion, again on the basis of Art. 4 of the preliminary provisions, then, the only argument that could help, if not to remove, at least to ward off possible objections reads as follows. The state of necessity gives rise to the right of the state to issue the dispositions in which the state of siege is actualized. It matters little that these dispositions coincide with those expressly included in the military penal code for the state of war – this is a simple accidentality that in the abstract could also not occur. Rather than an interpretative extension of these latter norms, it amounts to the issuing of new norms, although they are identical to others that apply to other cases (which allows one to limit oneself to a simple reference). Up to this point, the argument could be correct. But a problem inevitably resurfaces when one wonders what the state derives this right from. Given that necessity, according to the theory that I am refuting, is not itself a source of law, evidently, another source must be found that gives it these effects. One should rule out customary law, quite understandably and for the reasons that I will discuss below; one should also rule out an explicit legal provision, which is nowhere to be found; and one should finally rule out the possibility of extending a provision on a similar subject by analogy. Thus, one is left but with the expedient of the so-called general principles. But this expedient seems to me even less admissible. For if it results in the so-called *analogia iuris*, I fail to understand how, in the case of an exceptional circumstance and of a matter involving restrictions on individual freedom, one can have recourse to such an analogy when the *analogia legis* is believed to be impossible. The reason that prevents the *analogia legis*, Art. 4 of the preliminary provisions, also prevents the *analogia iuris*, which is a more remote analogy. There is no doubt about that. And it would be strange if this were not the case. If it is true that, according to the doctrine in question, we are called upon to solve the problem by keeping within the boundaries of the law as it arises from the system of legislation, then it is not altogether clear why we should turn down the aid offered by a proximate provision to turn to norms that are so remote that they are often elusive, as the so-called general principles are. I'd like to go even further. The right to extend exceptional and restrictive provisions beyond the cases expressed in them implies by logical necessity the assumption that in this matter no general principles, in the sense of Art. 3 of the preliminary provisions, are possible, but only specific and concrete norms.

30 *On the Decree Laws*

Before drawing the inevitable conclusions from what I have argued so far, a more detailed examination of the theory to which I have alluded will be useful. I will consider its latest formulation, the one offered by Ranelletti, which is undoubtedly the most valuable and the most precise.

According to this writer,[8] it is the concept of the state of necessity that we should refer to. For it implies the condition in which a subject may find himself protecting his own right, or that of others, against an imminent danger, or fulfilling a legal duty, only through the violation of another's right. This condition can take on various forms, some of which are not relevant to the issue of the state of siege. Thus, contrary to what has sometimes been affirmed, it would be incorrect to compare it to legitimate defence. For it does not only imply an action aimed at repelling an actual and unlawful attack, but also affects all the people who live in a given territory, even those who did not attack anybody. The state of siege would thus be an aggressive state of necessity whereby one is forced to violate the sphere of activity of individuals who are not causing the danger that is jeopardizing the law of the state. The principles governing the state of necessity would be so broad and based on such general grounds that they should be applied in all fields of law, even though provisions expressly referring to it are only to be found in criminal law. Thus, as far as the state of siege is concerned, a collision surfaces between 'the state's right, and even its fundamental and absolute duty to defend and guarantee its existence and its legal order, and the right of individual liberty and the guaranties which the order itself recognizes and protects, to the extent that the one cannot be saved without jeopardizing the other.' In this condition, the general principles of the state of necessity are alleged to justify the governmental act imposing such restrictions on individual rights. In the state 'one must recognise a true subjective right of necessity, and in the governmental act, which constitutes its exercise, a fully legitimate act.' A search 'in our legislation' is claimed to lead to attributing such effectiveness to necessity.

It is my opinion that such a line of reasoning cannot be followed. To begin with, I believe it improper to compare the kind of necessity that yields certain effects in the area of criminal law or even private law[9]

---

8   Ranelletti 1904, 1182 ff.; 1201 ff.
9   See Lombardo-Pellegrino 1903, 3 ff. The author believes that for a theory of the decree-laws and the state of siege 'it is sufficient to extend to public facts the concept of necessity that has been developed in private law' (128). However, his conclusions are opposite to Ranelletti's, in that he accepts the doctrine that does not find in such measures any legitimate manifestations

On the Decree Laws 31

with the kind of necessity that can give rise to a state of siege. This is all the more true insofar as it is a mistake to believe that the essential characteristic of the state of siege is the conflict that arises between the right of the state to preserve its existence and political structure and the individuals' right to freedom, which must be limited or sacrificed to the advantage of the former. This clash between the two rights is and cannot be but a secondary aspect, a simple consequence of a more general and comprehensive dynamic. On the other hand, this observation is targeted not only against the theory that I have just hinted at, but also against the tendency, which has always been particularly strong, to emphasize the restrictions that the state of siege brings to individual liberties more than anything else. Perhaps this should be regarded as a residue, though inadvertent, of the erstwhile constitutional doctrine that took this freedom to be an irreducible *prius*, a more or less impenetrable barrier to the power of the state. However, what matters here is that what characterizes and distinguishes the type of necessity that leads to the state of siege is, first and foremost, the material and absolute impossibility of applying, under certain conditions, the norms that regulate the normal life of the state, as well as the need, not to apply other existing norms, but to issue new ones. Thereby the consequence that the original moment, which must be taken into consideration, is precisely this substitution, albeit provisional and limited, of a new law [diritto obbiettivo] for the law [diritto obbiettivo] that already exists. If individual freedom is restricted, suspended, unprotected, this is not the immediate consequence of any right of the state, but of the new and exceptional legal order that the state sets up and that redetermines the respective boundaries of the power of the state and the activity of individuals. What must be explained and justified, then, is nothing other than the state's power to establish a procedure that is not the usual procedure for issuing new norms. Now, while searching for the foundation of this power, it is incorrect and one-sided to concentrate on the freedoms of citizens and, more in general, on their rights. The problem is more serious and more complex: what one should look at is the constitution of the state as a whole, the distribution of competences among the various constitutional bodies, the position and reciprocal relations between these bodies, a number of fundamental principles that refer to the

of a legal power of the state, and regards them as barely factual measures that can also be justified, and yet remain outside of the law. Therefore, although I think his theory is not acceptable (see below), it escapes the objections that I raise against Ranelletti's.

32 *On the Decree Laws*

constitutional order of the state itself. The rights of citizens are contingent on this order: if the latter is modified, even temporarily, there is no doubt that these rights, too, can be modified, restricted, or suppressed; conversely, if the order cannot be modified, restrictions cannot be considered but illegitimate. It is not the right of the individual that determines the constitutionality of a norm, but the intrinsic characteristics of the norm itself, which conversely determines the consistency and extension of that very right. If this is the case, it looks beyond doubt that it is improper to consider the imposition of a state of siege as the exercise of a right of the state as opposed to the right of the citizen. The type of necessity that, for certain effects, lies within the scope of criminal law or private law can well be reduced to a simple opposition between two rights: the existing legal order allows one of them, under certain extraordinary circumstances, to prevail over the other. But as far as the state of siege is concerned, it is the legal order that must be established in the first place. Indeed, as the theory I examined above implicitly and insistently affirms, the measure of the state of siege is the enactment of legal norms, the exercise of the legislative function, to employ its lexicon. To repeat: the state bears no right that could be exercised against that of the citizens unless the state attributes this right to itself by means of a new norm. The relationship between the former and the latter is therefore mediated by such an element; or better, it does not arise before it occurs. Here lies the irreducible difference between the two cases, which prevents applying to the one the principles of the other.

Alternatively, my claim can be vindicated in another way. Imagine – and clearly here the degree of probability bears no importance vis-à-vis the abstract possibility itself – that, in order to put down a revolt, instead of resorting to the measure of the state of siege, a temporary governmental provision is issued, one that is meant to extend, rather than restrict, the freedom of the citizens to let the situation cool down and remove the cause of discontent. This is a hypothetical case in which, if one intends to provide the grounds for this measure, one must have recourse to necessity, as is the case with the state of siege; but it is clear that the concept of necessity that determines a state of siege cannot be likened to this hypothetical case, since there is no conflict with the rights of individuals, no limitations on those rights, no overriding on the part of state law, and so on. And yet, the two figures are perfectly similar – indeed it is one same figure that can appear under different guises. The reason for this is that with regards to the state of siege one places emphasis on an element that is not essential to it – one that, when it obtains, is altogether secondary, and may even be lacking at all.

On the Decree Laws 33

Again, and to return to a line of reasoning that I have already addressed, it is easy to see how, with respect to the state of necessity, insofar as it implies a conflict between two rights, it is possible to go beyond the explicit provisions of the law to formulate general principles with the aid of *analogia legis* or even *iuris*. In substance, these are not restrictive norms, because they merely balance two rights; nor are they exceptional norms, although they cover a case that is less common if compared to more frequent cases. The exceptionality of the norm is to be measured against that which it provides for the case it regulates, and not against the case itself: the exceptionality of the norm is one thing, the extraordinariness of the case is another, while a plainly ordinary case may well be tackled with an exceptional norm. But when a state of siege is at stake, if we want to give Art. 4 the meaning that is usually and unanimously given, I fail to understand, based on what I argued above, how one can rely on a general principle, deduced with the aid of *analogia iuris*, especially once the *analogia legis* with the military penal code has clearly proven inadmissible. Here we have not only a case, but a norm – one that is claimed to authorize the state of siege, which is completely exceptional and restrictive. While this norm cannot be found in an explicit form, it cannot even be found in an implicit form, when one looks for it in legislation.

From this point of view, other theories may look more logical: both those that absolutely do not recognize the measure of the state of siege and, more generally, the decree laws, and those that, while not admitting any right or any law of necessity, do not exclude that sometimes necessity can be invoked as a factual element and, although it remains outside of the law, can have some effect in the legal field (this is especially meant to exonerate from all responsibility those who have enacted or executed acts which, though illegitimate, are by necessity itself politically justifiable).[10] But neither of these views looks acceptable to me. The former is too simple and the latter quite artificial. Especially insofar as they have been deduced from the law of other states, the former and the latter are at variance with the needs of real life and appear more as manifestations of theoretical and personal views than

---

10 I am putting together these opinions for what they have in common and am not pointing out the divergences whereby each takes on a character of its own that is not relevant for my purpose. I also omit any quotation (for references, see Ranelletti's and Gmelin's works). In fact, the opinions to which I am referring are often underdeveloped and sometimes developed in a contradictory way, so much so that I would need to justify for each one why I think that it should be associated to the others. This would take too much for an occasional writing like the present one.

34   *On the Decree Laws*

as the deep scrutiny and the precise formulation of the *ius quo utimur*. In fact, it seems impossible to exclude from the field of law the manifestation of powers which the law tends to regulate and restrain. And perhaps it is not inappropriate to observe what follows. The theories I alluded to are most often, if not always, stimulated by the fear that, under the pretext of necessity, the arbitrariness of the government may infiltrate matters that should be governed by legal norms. However, their advocates fail to realize that, since it is not actually possible to prevent the government from exercising these powers, when they suggest that they are excusable, the idea that they lie outside of the law has no practical consequence other than to free them from all limitations and make them arbitrary even when they would not be.

The truth is that, quite apart from any consideration of this kind, each of the theories that I have discussed so far draws from a correct principle, whereas the divergences among them arise from the fact that they fail to see how they can be reconciled with each other about principles that are wrongly deemed to be opposed and mutually exclusive. The former theories start from the right observation that the state of siege and, in general, the powers of necessity of the government are, and can only be, juridical. Yet they are mistaken, as I have illustrated, in that they seek their foundation in the legislation and believe that all positive law is contained within it. The latter theories, on the other hand, rightly hold that none of our laws justifies these powers, and, again based on the same mistake that law [diritto] and statutory law [legge] are synonymous with one another, come to the unfounded conclusion that these powers are contrary to our law. Therefore, the only point that is worth stressing, because it is the real crux of the matter and the latent cause of disagreement, is the following: Is there, beyond legislation, any genuine source of law in which the powers of the government that are at issue here may find their root and legitimacy?

For a start, I think that the possibility that this source be customary should be excluded. Some scholars have conjured customary law to recognize their value,[11] especially in relation to the state of siege.[12] Even those who have not explicitly spoken of customary law have often

---

11 See, more recently, Gmelin 1907, 94 ff., who believes that Art. 6 of the Statuto contains an unconditional and absolute prohibition of the government's powers of necessity, but that for this part as well as for the other that only allows regulations for execution, and not the autonomous and delegated ones, it has by custom lost its effectiveness.

12 A reference to customary law, though very fleeting and discreet, can also be found in Rossi 1894, 14.

examined the 'precedents' from a point of view that seems intended to reveal their effectiveness in terms of customs. Other scholars,[13] on the other hand, have observed that it is true that there have been many instances of state of siege in the Italian constitutional history; and yet, these instances have not been so frequent and have lacked the adequate degree of awareness about the juristic and lawful nature of the activity, which are elements of customary law. But beyond these arguments, which remain debatable, especially with regard to the *opinio iuris* with which the powers of the government are or are not claimed to be exercised, I think that a custom not only does not exist, but cannot exist because of the nature itself of the matter at stake.

First of all, I would like to observe what follows. Just like an exceptional and restrictive law cannot be generalized beyond the cases it covers, the norms enacted by the government to cope with an extraordinary event, marked by a high degree of exceptionality and temporariness, cannot be considered elements of a custom, and therefore have no value beyond the event to which they refer. Second, it should not be forgotten that an essential trait of the concept of the measures I am discussing is the assumption that they are legally permissible only if they are determined by necessity. If this is true, then the consequence is that customary law has nothing to do with them. On one side, the exercise of such powers cannot extend beyond what is strictly necessary by invoking a broader custom. On the other, and conversely, if customary law grants powers more limited than those which, in a particular contingency, prove to be necessary, the government cannot be prevented from exceeding those limits. Based on precedents, had they a customary value, one would have to assume, for example, that the extent of the state of siege could only be determined by an uprising: but the present case is the practical demonstration of the inconsistency of such a restriction.

The truth is that we must not forget a principle that seems commonsensical, especially if it is summarized in the aphorism that has become popular: 'Necessitas non habet legem.' The necessity that I am concerned with must be conceived as a state of affairs that, at least as a rule and in a complete and practically effective way, cannot be governed by previously established norms. But if it has no law, it makes law, as another widespread expression tells us. This means that necessity is itself a genuine source of law. And it should be noted that its value is not restricted to the special case of the urgency powers of the government, but is much wider and has much more significant and

---

13 Cammeo 1898, 13 ff.; Gamberini, 1903, 25 ff.; Racioppi 1909, 367; etc.

36 *On the Decree Laws*

general manifestations.[14] Necessity can be considered to be the first and original source of all law, so much so that, with respect to it, the other sources are somewhat to be considered as derivative. In the structure of contemporary states, which has evolved over such a long period and has reached such a remarkable degree of completeness, the normal production of law is usually fixed by a written norm. Thus, when one investigates the mandatory foundation of a norm, this foundation is to be found in an earlier norm establishing what bodies are authorized to enact it as well as their powers. But clearly, this investigation is destined to end the moment one arrives at a basic norm, which derived its force only from the necessity that brought it about. And in necessity must be found the origin and legitimation of the legal institution *par excellence*, that is, of the state, and in general of its constitutional order, when it is established by a *de facto* procedure, for example by a revolution. And what occurs at the initial moment of a given regime can also be repeated, albeit exceptionally and with more attenuated characteristics, even when it has stabilized and regulated its own fundamental institutions. In other words, a given state of affairs can occur that constitutes an explicit, urgent, and categorical manifestation of needs and social forces. Put otherwise, a compulsory norm immediately and directly emanates from it, with no uncertainty and no possibility of escaping it: it is a fact that, by its very nature, presents itself with the characteristics of law; it is necessity, the first source of the latter. Hence, whereas all positive law is believed to consist of legislation and custom, it is a mistake not to include necessity in the so-called unwritten law. Necessity shares with custom the character of a direct manifestation of social forces, but it differs from customary law in the greater energy and definiteness of the norm that derives from it, as well as in its immediate effectiveness, which does not need a period of time of varying length to be consecrated as such. Necessity is always urgent and pressing. The recognition of this source of law cannot be regarded as a residue of natural law theories:[15] while natural law would always consist of more or less rational norms, and has always been conceived as such, necessity, as we have seen, imposes itself more stringently; necessity does not take shape as a rational requirement, but as an entirely practical command, and, above all, is translated into

14 I have dealt with some of them in other writings. See Romano 1901 and Romano 1902, 23.
15 This seems to be what Ranelletti (1904, 1206) believes when he maintains that my theory, which I had already briefly mentioned in Romano 1898, cannot be accepted if one wants to 'remain and reason within the field of positive law.'

institutions [istituti] and norms that are enforced by state bodies. We are thus undoubtedly in the field of a law which is more strictly and properly positive.

We still need to explore the relation of necessity to the other sources of law, especially to statutory law, since customary law was considered above. We can disregard a few figures in this relation. Thus, it is pointless here to consider the case in which the law contemplates a state of necessity and seeks to regulate it. It is just as pointless to consider the other extreme case in which necessity begins to manifest itself as a force that menaces to destroy an entire legal order, for example, by a revolution, and from which no legal norms can evidently arise until it has successfully established a new political order. The only figure that is of concern here is the one in which there is a necessity demanding the non-application, albeit temporary, of a law and the temporary replacement of it by a new norm. Based on this hypothesis, on the one hand, one remains within the scope of the existing legal order; and this also derives from the consideration that this type of necessity implies the effects mentioned above insofar as it is aimed at defending the order from a hostile force, or at restoring its effectiveness, if this, for whatever reason, even involuntary, has ceased to exist, and is moreover felt and translated into contingent rules by the constituted powers. On the other hand, and as an inevitable consequence of what I just said, it is asserted *contra legem* in that legislation does not provide for a norm that regulates it or recognizes its efficacy. Therefore, the formula, which I have defended elsewhere, that the state of siege, in Italian law, is a measure contrary to the law, let us say illegal, but at the same time conforming to positive unwritten law, and therefore juridical and constitutional, seems to be most correct and convenient. The idea that necessity can overcome the law derives from its very nature, and from its original character, both from a logical and historical vantage point. Certainly, statutes have by now become the most discernible and general manifestation of the legal norm, but people go too far when their domain is extended beyond the field that pertains to them. There are norms that cannot be written down or should not be written down;[16]

16 This has often been pointed out even with regard to the state of siege. Thus, some have stated that it rests on 'a law that is prior to any law or Statuto' (Atti della Camera dei Deputati, Discussioni, session of 28 February 1894); that the state's necessity is a law that is not written because it is felt (Arcoleo, in the session of the Camera dei Deputati of 3 March 1894); that the law of necessity does not need to be declared, because it is self-evident and forms part of the 'common constitutional law' (Gmelin 1907, 91); that 'the necessary reality of things is the liveliest origin of every

38   *On the Decree Laws*

there are others that can only be determined when the circumstance arises that they are designed to deal with. In other words, written law can scarcely rule out unwritten law, and especially that part of it which is given by necessity and which in the highest degree possesses the *innata vis* which some people also assign to custom. For it to remain within the realm of positive law, as I noted, it is sufficient that it manifests itself as a force that defends and protects the existing order and is translated into commands of the state. If it manifests itself in the opposite sense, there is no denying that real law can arise from it. However, this will happen at a later stage, if and when it succeeds in constituting the power and the regime that will take it from the state of abstract justice to that of the state of concrete and stable order. Necessity can therefore give rise to legal measures, even when these are contrary to the law.

This *contra legem* character can occur in different degrees and forms. For example, we could hypothesize the existence of a statute providing for the possibility of any state of necessity, and despite this it could establish the general principle that, even in this case, only that statute is to be complied with, without any derogation whatsoever. Even in this case, I tend to believe that such a prohibition would be legally ineffective, and that necessity cannot be limited, let alone ruled out. It is well known that the same question applies to customs, which has often been maintained as legal admissible notwithstanding the opposition of the legislative. However, by dint of its greater energy and character, necessity would be able to overcome the latter more and better than customary law. For example, I do not think that its authoritative character fades out even when it relates to a case that the law has contemplated and regulated, such as the state of war: if the military authority or the government needed other powers than those allowed by the military penal code, assuming that the latter limits them, these powers would be juridically exercisable.

This implies that we are fruitlessly concerned with legislative provisions that according to some exclude any act enacted by the government *contra legem*, even in cases of urgent necessity. It may even be

legal act' (Rossi 1894, 14); that 'there is no need for written laws to prove the constitutionality of the state of siege; indeed, it is natural that written laws do not exist, etc.' (Rossi 1899, 19). As we can see, even though all these fleeting expressions often lack a more complete determination, even though they do not specify in what sense a law of necessity should be admitted (is it a right [diritto subbiettivo] or a law [diritto obbiettivo]?), and even though they are instrumental in the delineation of a genuine theory, they have considerable significance.

On the Decree Laws   39

true that Art. 6 of the Statuto Albertino, which obliges the King not to suspend the observance of the laws and not to dispense with them, is meant – and I think this is not the case – to provide for and regulate this extraordinary case in a negative manner. It may even be true that – contrary to what I think – no importance should be attached to the fact that in the drafting of this article the adverb 'never' was dropped, while it appeared in the corresponding article of the 1830 French constitutional chart.[17] In the case in question, one should also consider other well-known provisions, whose meaning I believe does not cover it, since they concern only common and normal cases: the rule, not the exception. These arguments prove nothing when one acknowledges the principle laid down above.

And indeed, one should consider that the state of siege, like any urgent decree law, when it is not positively permitted, is always and at all times contrary to the law. It all depends on which law. Its illegality will be more serious and, in any case, more evident and starker, when an explicit provision forbids it. But even when there is no such provision, it will be contrary to all laws in which there are norms that do not contemplate the case of necessity and thus could not be legally overridden unless there is a higher source of law above them[18] – higher

17 As is well known, the importance of this deletion was emphasized by Codacci Pisanelli 1900, 96 ff., and rarely did those who have contested this importance correctly understand his thinking. He did not mean to say that, since the adverb 'never' was not included in Art. 6 of the Statuto, that article *allowed* emergency ordinances. Rather, he only wanted to say that it did not absolutely and expressly prohibit emergency measures, although it establishes a principle that, strictly interpreted, implies such a prohibition. The distinction could well be subtle, but the language of constitutional texts often is, for the sake of prudence and correctness, a kind of diplomatic language, which does not exclude voluntary reticence and mental reserve. And those who are aware of this know that this distinction obtains. Those who would like to examine the meaning of Art. 6 of the Statuto in relation to emergency measures in the light of the corresponding articles of constitutional charts that are anterior to ours may see Hatschek 1899; Spiegel 1907; Menzel 1908.

18 For it cannot be argued that if there is no provision in the laws that excludes necessity measures, it must be assumed that they are also admissible on the basis of the laws themselves. One could be led to this view by considering that necessity is such a source of law that cannot be generically disregarded, so that in practice this recognition can be assumed to be implicit until the prohibition becomes evident. This would always be countered by the principle that an exceptional and restrictive norm must be expressed as long as its basis is linked to a law; at least the legislative precept allowing it must be expressed. Only when one goes into the field of unwritten law does this principle no longer have any value and could not,

40   On the Decree Laws

than that by which acts having the force of law must be enacted with the concurrence of parliament, as well as all the innumerable others that can be provisionally replaced by the governmental decree. As far as Italian law is concerned, in my view, this second figure obtains: the illegality is, as it were, minor, but substantially similar to the more open one that would obtain in the other case mentioned above.

Once these principles have been established, it is relatively easy to solve the problem that, in the way it is commonly formulated, reminds me of the squaring of the circle. This is the problem of whether or not the act that declares the state of siege is a legislative or an executive act. The answer also depends on the meaning that is attributed to these expressions, which is not always precisely determined. Given that these are measures that do not have their grounds in existing legal norms, to which they are contrary, there is no doubt that they would normally fall within the competence of the legislative bodies, and therefore by their very nature are true legal norms. And this is so when they are used, as is the case with the state of siege, to enact new provisional norms, and also when they consist of special and concrete acts, as may be the case with many emergency decrees. Nevertheless, necessity operates precisely on this point: it alters the normal order of competences; it absobs into governmental tasks what would not be otherwise. The result will be an exceptional and extraordinary governmental competence, but always determined by a source of law, and therefore not a *de facto* and anti-juridical infringement of the competence of others.

This, however, does not rule out the possibility that the governmental act may be submitted to the legislative bodies for statutory approval. This consequence evidently follows from the character of necessity, since it is a derogation from the normal principle that attributes the exercise of the legislative function to the two Chambers and to the King. Exception to this principle is only admissible if it is justified by necessity, and since this is temporary, it follows that sooner or later the common competence must be restored over the extraordinary one, even to determine whether the latter was exercised legally. And several other reasons support this view.[19] Here I cannot even hint at them, nor can I examine the numerous and vexed questions that are related to it. It suffices for us to formulate the following corollaries, which can be deduced more or less directly from what I have so far said.

---

as is natural, materially have any value. Even this last resort to remove the inherent *contra legem* character of the state of siege and similar measures would therefore not stand up.

19 Among the many who have dealt with the subject, see Vacchelli 1898.

On the Decree Laws 41

A statutory approval *is to be* enacted in any case. It *may* be designed to recognize the existence of the type of necessity that justifies the governmental act and that is a prerequisite for its validity, without transforming this very act into law and allowing it to subsist in its original form.[20] Still, it *may* also have another objective. It may be designed to legalize an act that, when it was enacted, was juridical but *contra legem*. It is mistaken to believe that such conversion only applies to emergency measures that are permanent by nature, and therefore not to the state of siege, which is a transitory measure that ceases to be effective once the state of need ceases to exist. Indeed, it is easy to see that, even when the state of siege is lifted, its effects may persist – it will not continue to create new relationships, but those that it has already created may continue to exist. More than that, from these latter relationships new ones may arise – relationships that, not immediately but mediately, have their foundation in the decree proclaiming the state of siege. Its conversion into law is therefore just as justified as that of other, more permanent emergency measures. On the other hand, the Italian practice excludes such conversion for the state of siege; yet, not for this reason but for others that I will mention below, admits it for decree laws that are just as provisional, such as the so-called 'catenacci.' Finally, one should also consider the hypothesis that the parliament may recognize that necessity, when the state of siege was proclaimed, did call for exceptional measures, and yet it did not require governmental competences for such measures, because it was possible and even advisable to convene the Chambers. In this case the parliament may wish to deny that those measures, in so far as they were enacted by the government, were lawful, but at the same time may desire to maintain their effects as they are deemed to be intrinsically right and necessary, apart from the question of competence. So, the parliament itself would have enacted them. Evidently, in this case only a conversion into statutory law can achieve this end.

On this point, therefore, it is advisable to limit oneself to advancing one simple principle: it is necessary that the legislative bodies manifest their will by means of a statute. Its content may vary according to the various cases, the time at which it is enacted, and the circumstances. The statute may just ascertain the urgency of the governmental act and

20 This would be the only end that Ranelletti (1904, 1207 ff.) assigns the law of approval, which he also considers indispensable. I cannot follow him on this. Let us leave aside here the question of whether such a law is merely formal, as Ranelletti believes, or whether the criticism of his theory made by Gmelin (1907, 160 ff.) is well-founded.

42   *On the Decree Laws*

prove it without converting it into a law. It may operate this conversion either in case the government's act, which remains *contra legem*, was made legally admissible by the necessity that brought about the governmental competence, or in the opposite case, which I illustrated. It may be designed to release from all liability which may have arisen from the act itself and from its execution. It may also not affect this point, at least to a certain extent.

However, unlike some of the decree laws issued on the occasion of the Calabrian-Sicilian earthquake, the decree on the recent state of siege does not contain the clause of its discussion in the parliament; nor did this discussion take place when the Chambers were deliberately convened to deliberate on the measures relating to such a public calamity; nor does it seem likely that it will take place later. The practice that was constantly followed before 1898 has thus been resumed – which is to say, the year in which the state of siege proclaimed in various Italian regions gave rise to the law of 17 July, as is well known. This law seemed to uphold what the doctrine had almost unanimously and insistently formulated, and not improperly its importance was emphasized not only for the individual case to which it referred, but for the implicit recognition of certain principles that were believed to provide the grounds for it. The good example was not followed, however, and this is to be greatly deplored. Those who accept the theory that I have sought to develop about the nature of the act proclaiming the state of siege should not harbour any doubt about the need for a legislative pronouncement in the sense I illustrated above. But I think this is clear even if one follows the doctrine that the governmental practice has adopted, which holds that the powers of the government are based on the provisions of the military penal code, applicable and extensible to the civil state of siege. Indeed, since the element that legitimizes and makes such an extension possible is always the element of necessity, the declaration that this has materialized in the specific case can only transitorily fall within the competence of the government, but must subsequently be the subject of a specific legislative act. This is precisely what is asserted and coherently demonstrated by the doctrine that takes the measure on the state of siege to be grounded on general principles that are derived from our written law, from our laws.[21] And the same conclusion should be reached by those who look for the foundation of the measure itself, not in the existing body of laws as a whole, but in a particular law, such as the military penal code, which contemplates a similar case. I can see no reason why the

21   See Ranelletti 1904, 1207 ff.

two logically developed opinions should come to different conclusions on this point.

It should be noted that in the present case there has not been, and there will not be, any explicit and special vote of confidence,[22] which would sanction the government's measure insofar as this is possible in this way. On the other hand, this is but a logical application of the principle on which it is grounded, although it is an application that proves the groundlessness of this very principle. Unless one accepts that the extraordinary competence of the government is based on a motive that must be recognized and confirmed by the legislative bodies, it is not clear why the latter should, as a matter of political control, expressly vote on the conduct of the government itself. This control may well be exercised, but it could be exercised indirectly, and above all it will not be necessary to solicit it, given that the parliamentary situation is such as to imply, albeit tacitly, confidence in the Cabinet. Pushed to its extreme logical conclusions, the doctrine followed by the government's practice removes any guarantee of correct exercise from one of the most jealous and dangerous faculties. Within the constitutional frame, the powers of necessity can, or rather must, be considered as fully founded on positive law, and there is no need to worry too much about the fears of those who see in them a residue of the ancient absolute powers – a way to circumvent the norms that govern the representative system. Nevertheless, it is evident that this system and the principles on which it is based cannot be disregarded without mortally wounding them, without making them unable to achieve the end they must serve. Necessity may temporarily step outside legality, but legality must be restored when the effects of necessity end. Without this check and these limits, which derive from its very nature, one can hardly distinguish genuine necessity from arbitrariness and the unconstitutional confusion of powers. It is worth repeating: the ancient practice, improperly revived in the present case, frustrates the most legitimate hopes held by the doctrine – hopes that the doctrine, after the law of 1898, could believe not to be vain, with such an agreement on this point that seems to rule out any doubt.

Recently, some scholars have argued that, while necessity may justify the proclamation of a state of siege, it cannot determine further

---

22 During the sitting of the Chamber of Deputies on 31 March, there was a debate on the *general* policy of the Ministry, which led to a vote of confidence. In this debate, the Head of the Cabinet and a few opposition speakers made a quick reference to the measure of a state of siege for Messina and Reggio, but it does not seem, however, that the vote of the Chamber can refer to it.

44 On the Decree Laws

measures; let alone justify them. Consequently, in order to maintain, revoke or extend the state of siege, the government is called on to propose the relative bill to the parliament or obtain from it a delegation of powers.[23] It is true that some think it necessary to make an exception to this principle in the event that the parliament is not, and cannot be, convened in time; but even with this proviso, I do not think that the principle is fully vindicated. The general rule is that the authority that has taken a measure may also amend or revoke it. The limitation of the governmental competence on this matter could logically be defended by admitting that the proclamation of a state of siege by decree can only be made if and when the Chambers are not, and cannot be, convened. But I have doubts about this, as it is contrary to the Italian practice. Even when the parliament is convened and is in action, the government's powers cannot be ruled out. For it may be a type of necessity to which the government may be more sensitive than the Chambers. Moreover, the delay in the deliberation of the Chambers, which cannot be as prompt as a deliberation of the Ministers, may be hazardous. And as far as the lifting of the state of siege is concerned, it must be observed that the parliament may be well informed of the end of the state of necessity after the government, and ordinarily through it. Any hesitation related to this, as well as the inevitable delays typical of the legislative activity, however accelerated it may be, more often than not would prolong the state of siege beyond what is necessary, that is, beyond the period in which it can be justified. If the state of siege is maintained even one day only after its necessity has come to an end, it remains a measure with no legal basis, an unjustifiable arbitrariness. Based on this, I think that in the present case the government did right in revoking its decree, without involving the legislative bodies, though they were convened when the state of siege was in force.[24]

Numerous other crucial points could be discussed here, but the present essay has already overstepped the limits deriving from its purely occasional character. It is worth mentioning them briefly. First, as far as the content of the state of siege is concerned, the recent case shows how difficult, not to say impossible, it is to determine its precise limits. For example, in the territories of Messina and Reggio, the freedom of the citizens was subjected to an unprecedented limitation. Survivors were forced to evacuate, whereas in other circumstances only non-natives or at least non-domiciled or non-residents were driven out.

23 Ranelletti 1904, 1209, 1247. His opinion is followed by Gmelin (1907, 208 ff.).
24 Royal Decree No. 46 of 6 February 1909.

Furthermore, some believe that the state of siege only can entail preventive measures, which are typical of the function of the police; therefore, no part of the civil and commercial legislation could be modified or suspended based on the state of siege, although that has sometimes occurred.[25] In truth, this is highly questionable, and the state of affairs engendered by the earthquake in Calabria and Sicily, which disrupted all relations of ordinary life in such a way as to make all existing legal norms inapplicable, may serve to demonstrate that even in this area the powers of necessity have reason to be exercised. The government, in fact, employed a decree law[26] to extend the expiry date of certain debts and to suspend peremptory prescriptions and terms. However, while this measure was taken directly by the central government rather than the Royal Commissioner, it is not consequential to the state of siege. It can also be assumed that the path recently followed is preferable to the one adopted in previous cases. On the other hand, if the government had not taken action itself, I believe that the local Commissioner would have acted legitimately by issuing those provisions imposed by the most obvious necessity. Then again, the system that was adopted most probably depended on chance more than anything else: the decree law to which I am referring bears the date of 1 January and is therefore prior to the proclamation of the state of siege, although it was published afterwards, on the 7th. If this proclamation had taken place earlier, maybe the measure might have been taken by the Royal Commissioner.

However, the current case shines a light on a most relevant point; which is to say, the impossibility, according to the doctrine, for the state of siege to influence not only the organization and exercise of police functions, but also the organization and exercise of other public functions. This alleged impossibility looks unfounded, especially with regard to the attribution of jurisdiction to the military courts, which had been so vividly and, we may say, almost unanimously denied. In truth, I have nothing to object to those who seek to demonstrate that in the concrete cases that have occurred the institution of those courts went beyond necessity and could not therefore be justified. I am not concerned with this issue here. Rather, what must be excluded is that in all cases and as an absolute principle the jurisdiction of military courts is inadmissible.[27] Based on what I argued

---

25 Thus Maiorana 1894, 59 and 94; Ranelletti 1904, 1241; and others. Against this view, rightly, see Gmelin 1907, 201.
26 Royal Decree No 6 of 1 January 1909.
27 On this topic, see the correct considerations by Rossi (1894, 14 ff.). In the same vein, see also Gmelin 1907, 185 ff.

46   *On the Decree Laws*

above, it is pointless to rebut the arguments that draw from well-known provisions of the Statuto or other legal norms governing the exercise of the jurisdictional function in a way that is incompatible with that which would take place with these extraordinary and exceptional tribunals:[28] these provisions are part of the written law, which can be overcome and overwhelmed by necessity. However, other arguments are just as untenable, that is, those that seek to prove that the state of siege implies a condition in which the governmental authority, in order to save the law under threat, can limit or sacrifice the law of others, can act against existing things or against activities that are currently taking place or are about to take place, and yet cannot strike with jurisdictional acts those acts that have already been carried out and their authors.[29] In the previous pages, I have disputed the conception of the state of siege from which these consequences are drawn – the conception that improperly models the state of siege after a state of necessity in which individuals may find themselves in their mutual relations. The present case shows how necessary the institution of courts may be in addition to ordinary ones, whether these have ceased to exist or are unable to function. Indeed, this was one of the strongest reasons for the proclamation of the state of siege.[30] This may be a very special case, but it helpfully highlights how in such matters *a priori* criteria are doomed to lose all consistency in the face of the unpredictable manifestations that necessity may assume. Therefore, all that one can establish is the principle that lawful is everything and only what is necessary, giving up hope of fixing in the abstract what may or may not be necessary.

It is precisely from this point of view and for these reasons – and in this respect I agree with most Italian writers – that I have always considered inappropriate a statutory law regulating measures that, like the state of siege, escape any regulations other than those specific to the case to which they refer. If such a statutory law had been enacted – and the example of foreign legislations that have provisions on this subject

28 These arguments were mainly developed by Cammeo 1898, 5 ff., but are accepted by many other writers.
29 In this sense Ranelletti 1904, 1229 ff., 1233 ff.
30 Otherwise, it might have been possible to think of sending some commissioners with broad powers, so as to avoid, at least formally, the figure of the state of siege hitherto reserved for other contingencies. But it had the advantage of solving the serious problem of how the judicial function was to be exercised. Indeed, it was the only measure that could be adopted in order to have courts whose organization and operation had already been established. And it would have been impossible to improvise all the provisions that subsequently had to be enacted for the restoration of the ordinary jurisdiction.

On the Decree Laws   47

is significant[31] – one would hardly believe that it would have been so broad as to include the figure of the state of siege for a public calamity; it would only have provided for the hypothesis of revolt or some other similar hypothesis. I have already said, and it is worth repeating: it is a prejudice to believe that the law can extend so far as to eliminate completely that source of law which goes beyond and above it, that is to say, necessity. If one wants to force law in this sense, one in practice only demonstrates its impotence. Aspirations towards legality are undoubtedly healthy and respectful of the spirit of our public law; but they have an inexorable limit, however simple: that of the possible.

I would like to say a few words about one last point. As is well known, a very delicate and difficult problem is that of the jurisdiction of ordinary courts in the face of decrees issued by the government in the exercise of its powers of necessity, whether they take the form of a state of siege or involve other measures. Based on what I have stated, it is implicit but evident that I cannot accept the opinion that grants the government these powers but believes that the judge, because of their *contra legem* character, should abstain from applying them. In that case, should it prove necessary, the government might perhaps not execute judgments unfavourable to its own acts, could impose obedience to the judges with coercive force, but could not expect the jurisdiction to come to its aid and recognize the acts. This opinion could be accepted if one endorsed the view – and not even in all its various formulations – that alleges necessity to be a state of things that assigns the government a barely *de facto* power or justifies the exercise of such power in spite of its anti-legality. Quite the contrary, I have tried to show that the government measures enacted out of necessity are contrary to the law, but conform to a true source of law, that is, necessity. Consequently, I must admit that the judge may, indeed must, apply and recognize them, because he applies not only statutory laws, but all law, whatever its source. He is not in a position to judge whether or not necessity occurs in a specific case without invading the competence of the government, whose statements he must consequently trust. I think there is only one limit on this obligation, namely, when the

---

31 The French law of 4 April 1878, Art. 1, admits the state of siege in time of peace only in the case 'd'une insurrection à main armée'; the Prussian law of 4 June 1851, Art. 2, only in the case of revolt (*Aufruhr*); so does the constitution of the German Empire of 16 April 1871, Art. 68. In Italy, in 1894 the idea was that of including a provision on this subject in the military penal code. The formula that was considered as appropriate was broader, but in any case, either insufficient or insignificant: the state of siege could be proclaimed 'in case of insurrection or imminent danger to the public peace.' See the excellent considerations of Rossi 1894, 35 ff.

48　*On the Decree Laws*

act qualified as a decree of necessity includes in its intrinsic and objective elements something that allows the judge to ascertain that the decree is not actually based on necessity.

In this case, the judge would not be overstepping the bounds of his judicial role, but simply observing that the government's statement is contradicted by its own act; not an assessment of merit, a political judgment, but a legal examination of the act under scrutiny. This would be the case, for example, if the justification of a decree law referred only to reasons of convenience and expediency, not necessity; or a decree law whose application is fixed for a time more or less distant from the day of its enactment: necessity must be urgent, and this urgency would be denied by the government itself if it postponed its execution the very moment the decree law is enacted. Similarly, a decree law bearing a date considerably earlier than that on which it was published could be considered unconstitutional by the judge, and thus he could exclude the possibility that the government was driven by necessity when it expressed its will. And so on. But save for this case, I think the judge's duty to enforce decree laws is absolute. The inconsistencies that one would be faced with in adopting the contrary opinion[32] are emphasized by the present one better than other cases. For the provisions issued by the government after the Calabrian-Sicilian earthquake, as I pointed out time and again, go beyond the scope of the police, as they regulate a whole series of relations in the ordinary and even the private life of the citizens. They might not have had any practical effect if the government had relied only on material force to back them; if the judge had not been able to apply them and enforce them when necessary.

And with these remarks, which should certainly be developed further than what I can do here, I could close the present study, which has glossed over too many problems and could barely mention many others. However, it is also worth mentioning the exceptional measure that was adopted by Royal Decree No. 5 of 3 January 1909 in the district of Palmi, where no state of siege was proclaimed. In order to co-ordinate the civil and military services under the same command and to make the assistance to the municipalities damaged by the earthquake more effective and prompt, a Royal Commissioner was appointed, to whom all the authorities and

---

32　Gmelin's (1907, 103) observation that, if it were true that decree-laws were not also imposed on the courts and could not be applied by them, the government, instead of issuing decrees, could limit itself to issuing simple instructions to its officials and appealing to the goodwill of the citizens, is both correct and witty.

officials in the same district were subjected. This measure would not be particularly interesting in itself, and there are precedents in the past,[33] but these had to do with police measures in the strict sense, rather than a public calamity. However, it is worth noting that not even for this decree law, even though it was not covered by the powers attributed to the government by the Military Penal Code, is there a clause stating that it is to be submitted to the parliament. Some might have thought that, if submission to the parliament is not necessary for the Royal Decree proclaiming the state of siege, it is all the less necessary for a decree that establishes a measure of smaller gravity and that would be included in the Royal Decree. But for the reasons mentioned above, this is a line of reasoning that I cannot accept.

---

33 See Royal Decrees Nos. 142, 143, 144, 145 of 4 May 1898; 149 of 7 May 1898, and 157 of 9 May 1898, which concentrated police powers in the military authorities in some regions, placing prefects and other civil authorities under them.

2 The Modern State and its Crisis

Every science finds in its own nature and the procedures that appertain to it some particular and specific cause for mistakes. But possibly no sphere of human knowledge lumps together so many and perennial sources of delusions as the one that deals with the study of political institutions. These are phenomena of which it is even difficult to provide a description, because their form often conceals and distorts their substance and also because they take multiple and at the same time elusive appearances, as they stem from the continuous and never reconciled struggle between irreconcilable principles. Those that would seem the most reasonable expectations are often unsettled by the emergence of new elements, which manifest themselves all of a sudden, even when they have been prepared by age-old processes; by the combination and fusion of streams that are very distant from each other; by unpredictable historical recurrences; by deceptive mirages whereby one frequently comes across institutions whose life is only fictitious or whose death, on the contrary, is only apparent. And yet, even these phenomena are governed by laws, at the head of which is the one whereby the law and the constitution of a people are always the genuine product of its life and its inner nature. Famously, this is how this law was formulated by the founder of the historical school of law at a time in which, from the sudden upheaval of all political relations and from the formidable shock that shattered an entire world, the modern state arose, as if detached from the past, almost as creation *ex nihilo*. The violent crash of the French Revolution and its aftershocks tore apart institutions that had been elaborated by the age-old spirit of the various nations. It seemed as if the new institutions that emerged out of their ruins had been brought about by the magic wand of capricious legislators, under the auspices and dictates of goddess Reason, which at first sight could have paid a better tribute to such a name, made no less divine by the poets. A wit not as profound as Savigny's would have

DOI: 10.4324/9781003347774-3

The Modern State and its Crisis 51

been led astray by the following remark, which has recently been the object of criticism of his theory – which is to say, that very often public law, and sometimes also private law, is not the spontaneous product of the evolution of a people, but the outcome of a struggle. This outcome is only determined by material force, whether this struggle is fought within the state or between states, one of which imposes its law on the others, in a more or less disguised manner. According to those scholars, Savigny's doctrine, advanced when the contingent and the casual were celebrating their most typical triumphs with a series of events, is rooted in a romantic sentiment. This is the desire to get a foothold in the face of the general collapse, one that could allow the dismayed souls to hold onto the belief that the wisdom of the past had not been vain and that the new could be reunited to the antique, bent but not uprooted by the storm. In this way, Savigny is alleged to have proven once again that human beings never see what is close to them and happens before their eyes, or rather do not want to see it, in order not to move their gaze away from the more seductive spectacle of the stars. Rousseau charged Grotius with relying on poets; Savigny could be charged with being a poet himself. Yet, no charge has ever been more undeserved than this. It is especially worth pointing it out at a time in which it could acquire a special value and add one more argument to those by which, both in the doctrine and in the practice, the edifice of the modern state is being assaulted from all sides.

If it were possible to break down political institutions into the various elements that comprise what could well be called the public law which is common to most of the existing civilized states, they could be classified in three distinct categories. In these three categories, one should certainly make room – in a sense that I will describe shortly – for the reception of foreign law as well as for the influence exercised by largely theoretical currents. But the first of these categories should include all those principles and institutions [istituti] that are an immediate and direct emanation of the new forms of social structure which, although they manifested and imposed themselves through revolutionary means, are undoubtedly the result of a slow and gradual process of which the revolution was only the acme. The greatest and hopefully most durable characteristic of the modern state, whereby it appears as the sole source – if not the sole subject – of every public power, has precisely this origin. And as Art. 3 of the 1789 Declaration of the Rights of Man and of the Citizen proclaims and formulates its principle, in fact it did no more than articulate a legal situation that was emerging and definitely imposing itself in all evidence. The mediaeval state was long gone. Its various parts often fighting each other,

52 *The Modern State and its Crisis*

as is well known, could not merge into a complete unity. Therefore, each considered itself to be the depository by its own virtue and original right of at least a fraction of public sovereignty. Through a long chain of events and through infinite and subtle changes in the social fabric, both economically and morally, a principle consolidated and imposed itself, one that first appeared vigorously, but not fully matured, in the so-called police state, and then culminated in the figure of the modern state. This is the principle that the state, vis-à-vis the individuals who compose it and the communities that comprise it, is an entity *in se* that produces a unity out of the various elements of which it is made up of. At the same time, this entity should not be confused with any of these elements, in that it has a personality of its own, endowed with a power that descends from its very nature and its force, which is the force of law. Only in this way can it surpass the transient existence of individuals, even though it is composed of human beings. The state rises above non-general interests, and thus reconciles and harmonizes them. It puts itself in the position to take care not only of the present generations, but also of the future ones, and thus reconnects different instances and energies in an intimate and uninterrupted continuity of time, activities, and ends, so much so that it becomes an inclusive and typical expression of them. The Commune of our Risorgimento accentuated, in a series of institutions and under its own name, the aim of representing the interests of a community at large. Yet, it never came to the concept, though it was affirmed by romanists and canonists of the Middle Ages, that the community could be something different from its individual members. Therefore, it never gave life to a body superior to the collectivity itself, in a concrete and contingent sense. The police state also failed to come to this abstract conception. Although its fusion was greater, a kind of dualism remained between the state and the prince, who from time to time proclaimed himself master or servant of the state, depending on whether *de facto* the old principle was dominant or the principle that was about to emerge. The impersonality of public power, or better, the personification of power by means of the state, which itself was conceived as a person – this is the fundamental principle of modern public law: an immaterial but real person. It is an entity that is not fictitious or imaginary, but which, although it has no body, succeeds by means of delicate and marvellous juristic devices in forming, manifesting, and imposing its own will. It is not a shadow or a spectre, but a true principle of life, which does not operate by means of an organism in the true and strict sense of the word, but with the aid of a set of institutions adapted and harmonized for this purpose. This is a marvellous creation of the law, which according to a simplistic criticism

The Modern State and its Crisis 53

has no consistency other than that of a poetic fantasy. Instead, it is the fruit of a long and steady historical process that has given rise to a social magnitude, as it were, greater than any other and more active and powerful than any other. It is due to the state that individuals and collectives who in fact exercise sovereignty, in doing so, do not act as the holders of a right of their own, but as organs of the state, whose supreme will they express and implement, as impersonal agencies. His Majesty has no feet, observed Mirabeau. He alluded to this impersonality when the Constituent Assembly wanted to submit something to the king. Neither the monarch nor any assembly – even when it derives its origin from the people – could any longer repeat Louis XIV's famous phrase: 'I am the state,' let alone are there persons or communities that are above or outside the state. The state thus appears, and intends to be, not the object of domination, not the organ of a class, a party, a faction that holds sway because of a right proceeding from victory or power, but a complete synthesis of the various social forces. It is the highest expression of the cooperation between individuals and groups of individuals, short of which there is no well-ordered society. It is the supreme regulatory power and therefore a powerful means of balance. Even when in practice its institutions [istituti] become corrupt and degenerate, and the inevitable, permanent struggle between the objective force of law and the arbitrary force [potenza] of those who have power [potere] tends to be resolved in favour of the latter, it is always a great advantage and a great progress that all this can only be seen as a state of affairs which, far from being consecrated and recognized by the legal order, it turns out to be in opposition to the latter.

However, it seems that lately such an enlightening conception of the state, whose developments and applications I cannot examine here, has been obscured by an eclipse, which is intensifying by the day, to such an extent that it might not be entirely superstitious to draw unhappy omens from it.

And, indeed, I should mention here that there are doctrines that abstain from any political purpose and do not intend to change the present institutional order, which they only wish to describe and define exactly. Nonetheless, they deny that the state, even in its present form, can be considered as an abstract entity endowed with its own individuality and personality, as I described above. This would be nothing but a useless and superfluous legal fiction. On a closer look, reality always shows us an opposition between the governed and the governing, while public power is more and more centralized, not only factually but also juridically, in a more or less large number of physical

54 *The Modern State and its Crisis*

persons: in the prince, in the electors, in the elected, and so on. The state as an entity, the true Briareo with a hundred arms, or better with innumerable organs, is alleged to exist only in the imagination of somehow philosophically minded jurists, while a truly positive doctrine should not make room for any reality other than human beings. Quite a strange way of conceiving reality, which, to reiterate a famous comparison, could correspond to the reasoning of those who deny the existence of $\sqrt{2}$, just because in the world of natural phenomena nothing corresponds to it, or of *The Transfiguration* by Raphael in that the physicist can see in it only a piece of canvas and some colours. However, without the aid of too technical arguments, in this context it is not possible to show the inanity of such theories, which call themselves empirical whereas they are only naïve. But maybe it is not useless to observe that those who care to explore them could probably see the inadvertent and unconscious infiltration of tendencies that are not merely speculative and rather reflect a few instances that agitate today's social life. For it is often the case that the jurist, even an expert, who sets out to describe only positive law, whatever this may be, sees institutions through the deforming prism of the ferment of ideas and energies that press upon them.

However, we should relocate on less uncertain and less formal ground and should mention a general movement that aims at undermining not the scientific formula that defines the modern state, but the very foundations of its substantial principle – which is to say, a movement that, at least in its objectives, is more practical than theoretical, although it sometimes takes its cue from the doctrine.

Probably, the movement to which I am alluding is made up of many and varied energies. Some of them are so faint that they are hardly discernible, and yet, perhaps because of this, they often merge, so that, taken as a whole, they present themselves as a grandiose and interesting phenomenon.

A renewed sense of imperialism fuels this current, or at least, it gives it a certain aspect without contributing either to its creation or to its acceleration. At times, this very sense of imperialism denies the *raison d'être* of the law and thus of the modern state, which affirmed itself as a juridical state in the first place. At other times, it argues that it is right for the institutional order to turn into a kind of code of force. Says the Sophist Thrasymachus: 'In truth, justice is nothing but the advantage of the stronger.' These words could be placed as an epigraph to the writings of well-known modern philosophers and politicians. The existing state – and this is a typical feature of it – equates before the law the weak and the strong, the humble and the mighty, while it

The Modern State and its Crisis   55

should follow and reflect the instincts of conquest, of heroism, of the struggle between individuals, between the different classes, and between the different races. It is a deterioration to seek the collective welfare of a flock that is unworthy of it; it is a deterioration, therefore, a constitution that is not strictly and exclusively aristocratic, or rather, more exactly, oligarchic. And if I have here recalled these doctrines at their extreme and, as it were, monstrous formulation, we should not forget that they not only inspired the Dionysian philosophers. They can also be found, disguised under more positive appearances and with attenuated characters, in sociological conceptions, in truth very pedestrian, and yet not uncommon. And aside from any theoretical influence, the (unconscious but no less dangerous) feeling of exaggerated egoism and the lack of a concept of justice, which underlie these theories, manifest themselves in some instances of modern social life. Therefore, it could be useful to point it out. For if our times have emphasized those sentiments of equity, humanity, and solidarity, to which the supporters of heroic morality look with contempt, the fact remains that these sentiments risk being vain the very moment they should prove useful – which is to say, when social struggles intensify, as happens today.

It is precisely from these struggles, or rather from a special attitude they take, that the movement which is causing a kind of crisis in the modern state derives its maximum force. As we will see, within the state, and often against it, various organizations and associations are mushrooming and flourishing with a vibrant life and an effective power of their own. In their turn, these organizations and associations tend to unite and link together. They pursue disparate particular aims, but all of them have a common property: they assemble individuals based on the criterion of their profession or, better, of their economic interest. These are federations or syndicates of workers, industrial, mercantile, agrarian, and civil servants' syndicates; they are cooperatives, mutuality institutions, chambers of work, resistance or welfare leagues, all formed in keeping with the mentioned principle, from which they derive their collective form. This resurgence of corporatist tendencies on a professional basis, which were already so flourishing before they almost completely disappeared with the emergence of the modern state, has rightly been identified as the greatest fact of the contemporary age: it is, at least, the most general of all, the most certain and the most easily ascertainable. It is not an artificial movement, galvanized by more or less seductive doctrines. The latter play quite a secondary part in it, whereas its main source lies in the need for a firmer and more organic social fabric. This need is generally experienced, and naturally takes on a different consistency and colour depending on the way it

56   *The Modern State and its Crisis*

gets satisfied, but it is stimulated from all sides and supported by all parties. It is promoted and facilitated by those who aim to tip over the present order. Those who shun unconstitutional means and yet wish for deep and radical reforms look upon it with sympathy, as a powerful affirmation of democratic vitality. It is advocated, even officially, by the Catholic Church, which, especially with the encyclical *Rerum novarum*, proves to be highly favourable to corporatism. So, if we want to use the word 'syndicalism' to refer to this phenomenon, this term should be used in a very broad sense, and not only to designate workers' organizations, and even less so those of them that are more or less revolutionary. Regardless of how it came into life, the movement has now spread and has become generalized, and if it keeps any of its original attitudes, this is, in all probability, only contingent. In other words, it is the so-called integral syndicalism. Although it may or may not have kept its old name and although it is linked in some respects to its old manifestations, integral syndicalism is acquiring ever broader and more complex forms and manners.

I do not intend to trace either the historical origins or the economic foundation – which is certainly the most decisive – of this phenomenon. I will concern myself with it only as far as its direct consequences on the constitutional structure of the state are concerned. In the meantime, in its very affirmation, a presupposition is implicit by logical necessity: the fact that there is a need for new organizations, complementary to the state, if not contrary to it, is evidence that the existing state organization is insufficient. The long-standing and by now obvious observation that the political order which followed the French Revolution – like any other that is the product of a catastrophic upheaval – still carries with itself its original sin: that of being all too simple. This is the result of a reaction pushed to the extreme when the state came to believe it could turn a blind eye to a number of social forces. Either it deluded itself into thinking that they had disappeared, or it just took no notice of them, as it deemed them to be mere historical relics destined to vanish shortly. Worse still, the state often refused to recognize that which evidently still possessed an indestructible vitality. For it was afraid that such a recognition might provide the pretext for the re-establishment of the past. Once estates and guilds had disappeared and been suppressed, and even the Communes had been minimized, it was only the individual who was placed in front of the state. At face value, the individual was armed with an emphatically proclaimed and generously bestowed infinite series of rights, whereas in actual fact he was not always protected in his legitimate interests. There is no denying that the organization of the modern state, as far as

The Modern State and its Crisis 57

its affirming itself as the sole sovereign power is concerned, accurately reflected the new social structure. However, it soon proved to be totally deficient in regulating, indeed often in failing to recognize, the groupings of individuals that are so necessary in any society that has reached a high level of development. Unsurprisingly, social life, which is never dominated by legal rules, has continued to evolve as it saw fit, and mounted an opposition to a system that is at variance with it – and in doing so perhaps it accentuated the conflict and the struggle that result from it beyond what is necessary, as is usually the case.

In the meanwhile, if I had the time, it would be interesting to foreground how, little by little, and often without even realizing it, modern law has given in here and there. It modified itself, or has sought, when its provisions were a little dubious, to favour interpretations that could serve to avoid engaging further in a struggle that was disadvantageous to it, maybe to the detriment of accuracy. In this regard, one could recall the disputes that, although they pertain to the field of private law, originated from reasons of public order, concerning the legitimacy of industrial unions, disputes which are now being settled in favour of this very legitimacy. It could also be pointed out that in Italy associations of public officials are formed and live undisturbed, even those, for example, of magistrates, which could raise justified doubts. Be that as it may, typical and characteristic is the attitude of French positive law towards trade unionism. Famously, until a few years ago, French law held onto the principles that as early as 1791 had led to the dissolution of the art and craft guilds and had prohibited their reconstitution in any form. Despite this, the increasingly general and vital affirmation of workers' organizations had the law lessen these restrictive provisions, which it could not materially enforce without imposing criminal sanctions on a very large number of people. And where the legislator failed to operate, the juristic practice is gradually putting forward broad but debateable interpretations. Thus, while an authoritative doctrinal opinion denies civil servants' unions being permitted by the law of 1 July 1901, such unions are flourishing in huge numbers, the government proclaims their legality within the Chambers, and the Council of State goes so far as to affirm the capacity of such associations to take legal action against a measure of the authorities relating to the legal status of one of their members.

Therefore, modern public law does not dominate, but is dominated by a social movement, to which it is adapting with some difficulties, and which meanwhile governs itself with laws of its own. And while political writers are indulging, according to their different temperaments, in critical visions or discussions; while people are wondering if

58 The Modern State and its Crisis

we are lapsing back onto medieval guilds; while people are wondering if the existing trade unions are provoking an escalation of the social struggle and are pondering on their possible consequences on the energy of the individual character, the functioning of the public powers, the future of collectivism, and the general evolution of the economic world; while all this happens, the organizations of the various classes are multiplying prodigiously. And a great many of them, whether disguisedly or overtly, assume an antagonistic attitude towards the state. While the more moderate and conservative current affirms that professional bodies must be put under the guardianship and control of the state, it warns that they should never become its official instruments, and thus emphasizes, if not the character of opposition, that of independence. From other points of view, and as regards their practical attitude, there is no need to point out that all associations of this kind, for example those of civil servants, toy with the idea of acquiring a material power – one that can exert pressure on public powers, so as to obtain by the force that derives from their unification that which the state would never grant by listening to the voice of simple justice. In addition, sometimes, without reservation and without subtext, it is the substitution of the union's activity for that of the state that they demand. This is precisely the programme, in its most radical and revolutionary form, that worker syndicalism strictly speaking pursues. And in France, the civil servants' unions persistently claim they should participate in the general federation of labour: although their interests, which could be better protected through an autonomous organization, are divergent from those of the working classes, they share their anti-state purposes. One should only think of the famous manifesto of the syndicalist instructors, dated 24 November 1905, stating that 'the trade unions must prepare themselves to form the cadres of the future autonomous organizations, to which the state will entrust the care of ensuring, under its control and under their mutual control, the progressively socialized services.'

Nevertheless, if it is useful to identify the points on which the various corporatist movements tend to concur, it would be utterly erroneous not to differentiate the movement itself into two distinct currents. While both are nourished, as I pointed out, by economic factors, one of them emphasizes and amplifies them beyond measure and reaches extreme consequences; the other, conversely, pivots on a healthy idealism and does not forget that elements other than economic ones determine and consolidate all human achievements. The first of these currents is, of course, the simplest, indeed the most simplistic and, in its logic, disregards the precept 'cave a consequentiariis.'

The Modern State and its Crisis 59

In other words, this is Proudhon's conception of 'economic law' as superimposed on that of 'political law,' over which he claims a kind of primogeniture, which has been inverted only because of a historical illusion. The beginning and the end of any social organization is claimed to be the public economy, whereas the consideration of its needs is claimed to be not only necessary – which is beyond doubt – but also sufficient. Based on this, this current arrives – without any hesitation – at the decomposition of the modern state. The unity and the sovereignty of the latter is believed to have no reason to exist and to be destined to disappear: a whole chorus of voices, especially in France, raises this point and takes up the cry that Proudhon had already launched. Instead of the abstract sovereignty of the state, he foresaw

> an effective sovereignty of the ruling masses of workers, who will initially govern charity meetings, chambers of commerce, guilds of arts and crafts, workers' companies, stock exchanges, in markets, schools, agricultural committees, and finally electoral committees, parliamentary assemblies and state councils, national guards, and even churches and temples.[1]

The social organization is claimed to amount to the federation of these mutualist groups and, alongside them, by the municipalities and provinces. And yet, at present someone goes even further, and from this demolition does not even want to spare the municipality, the elementary political association, which we have always instinctively considered as necessary and to which we are bound by the most natural and strongest ties. According to Duguit, it has ceased to be 'a coherent social group!' Consequently, professional associations should not just take place alongside and together with those based on territorial and national ties – in other words, with political associations in the strict and etymological sense of the word – but could and indeed should do without them, whose value is considered as merely geographical. It is not one's birth, or a river or a mountain that should determine the cohesion of individuals. This is claimed to be better founded on productive force, trade, economic activities. The central power, much as it is needed, should soon reduce the scope of its action to simple control and surveillance. And this should be possible because the trade union movement, after a more or less long period of disruption and maybe violence, is supposed to be able to give the political and economic society of tomorrow a cohesion that our

1   [Romano's translation from Pierre-Joseph Proudhon, *De la capacité politique des classes ouvrières*, ed. by G. Chaudey, Dentu, Paris, 1865, 207.]

60 *The Modern State and its Crisis*

society has not known for centuries. It should be noted that these views are not held only by those who restrict the phenomenon of trade unionism to the working classes. They are shared by those who have arrived at the conception of a more complex and integral trade unionism, extended to all classes, that is, to all groups of individuals within a given society between whom there is a particularly close interdependence, in that they serve a function of the same order in the division of social labour.

And one could easily continue in this survey, which is not without interest, of the predictions on the corporatist organization of the future society that, through more or less fervent fantasies, grow by the day. Some, more prudent, declare that they do not wish to go too far in specifying the details of such an organization, as they do not aim to reconstruct a city of Utopia modelled after it. Yet others are oblivious to the recurrent experience that every social movement never follows a track that is completely traced from the beginning, but gradually breaks a path, whose length and point of arrival cannot be anticipated. Nonetheless, we must acknowledge that truth is quite a whimsical goddess, who often loves to conceal herself under the most fantastic appearances and never fails to peep, if only for a moment, behind phantoms and chimeras. It is then worth taking these into account and trying to see what is hidden beneath them.

The most indisputable kernel of truth that animates the modern tendencies towards corporatism lies in the fairly simple observation that the social relations that directly concern public law are not limited to those relating to the individual, on the one hand, and the state and smaller territorial communities, on the other. Doubtless, it would be totally at odds with the most evident and well-established historical process from which our civilization has emerged to ignore the latter. Yet, considering social organizations based on bonds other than territorial ones is just an elementary and fundamental requirement. And among these, the strongest and most spontaneous, indeed the most necessary, are, at least at present, determined by the economic interests of the individuals who compose them. Moreover, the distinction of society into classes is a phenomenon that can let up only transitorily, but never comes to an end. It may have seemed dangerous and contrary to public order when, on the one hand, the struggle between the various classes was alive and, on the other, the foundation of each of them could be considered extinguished or antiquated. But this is precisely one of those necessary phenomena which, once one of their manifestations comes to an end, inevitably finds another. The economic needs of modern society have thereby revived a distribution and organization of individuals that previously had different characteristics

The Modern State and its Crisis 61

and aims but is essentially a new phase of an ancient and perennial social requirement. From this point of view, it is obvious that corporatism, considered in its normal course and not in its degenerations, can serve to mitigate the harmful consequences of excessive individualism, which is the source of conflicts and struggles, to develop the feeling of solidarity between individuals, and the feeling of mutual respect between different groups of individuals, and thus to contribute to a more complete and compact social organization. And as far as the political constitution is concerned, we can hope that the corporatist movement will not aim to overthrow the state and the shape it has taken through modern law but to remedy the deficiencies and gaps that, as I illustrated, are a necessary effect of its origin. Indeed, we can hardly deny that a series of principles of present-day public law is not due to an exact translation into its system of imperative and clear social requirements, but precisely to the failure to take note of the latter. The state was either unwilling to recognize these requirements or unable to assert them at a time when a profound perturbation came to conceal them or to give them a shape that is not appropriate. Because of that, in order to complete the edifice of the modern state, foreign institutions [istituti] were adopted in the belief that English public law could be transplanted or imitated; by the same token, doctrinal principles that at the time appeared to be axioms of the most unquestionable natural reason provided fragile support. Fortunately, or rather by virtue of the principle that there is no true law that does not reflect an effective social condition – a principle that even in this case has not foundered, as one might superficially believe – the consequence of this was not the creation of institutions that were contrary to the new needs and requirements, but only the illusion of having created complete legal institutions. In reality, all that had been achieved were forms without content, schemes that were and still are to be filled. Modern constitutions do indeed claim to enshrine in their text all the fundamental principles of public law, but more often than not they have done no more than hint at institutions that then they failed to regulate, and write the headings of chapters that are not even sketched out. As a result, they have a far greater number of gaps than is generally believed. This was and is a good thing. For in this way the struggle that nowadays seems to be directed against them is likely to take on a different character if people realize that it is occurring in a field where there are no trenches to dismantle, but only defences to raise. To build and not to destroy: this is, more than anything else, the task that can and must be set, with respect to the political order, the evolution of our social life; and, once the new edifice has been built, it probably will no

62 *The Modern State and its Crisis*

longer be at variance with the solid and severe architecture of the modern state, but will rest on its very foundations and will constitute integral part of it.

For example, in the type of public law that is typical of the existing states, there is an institution [istituto] that elicits a very curious feeling: on the one hand, the belief that it is necessary and vital; on the other hand, the awareness that its purpose remains unfulfilled. No party, or almost no one, would do without it, but everyone is equally unhappy with it. It is the institution of political representation, which deserves mention here, as it is the one that in most respects has an unquestionable connection with my topic. For its aim is precisely that of linking the constitution of the state with that of society, the institutions with the mobile and fluctuating elements of public life. This explains why the advocates of corporatism have constantly turned their attention to it. But they have not always realized the meaning of that general sentiment to which I have alluded – which is to say, it is an institution [istituto] that need not be detached from the fundamental principles on which it rests. Rather, it has yet to acquire a positive content, inasmuch as it pursues an end that is, and must be, its own, but fails to attain it; it is the affirmation of a correct principle, but has no practical and effective regulation. Perhaps it is not useless to recall that political representation arose and acquired its characteristic shape in England, that is to say, in an order that did not forego, until very recently, the distinction of society into classes – a distinction that nevertheless leaves deep traces. However, being transported to a different political environment, its formerly decisive features have faded and almost disappeared. Famously, the most widespread opinion now affirms that what is called political representation only inexactly or, at most, by legal fiction retains such a name. In fact, in the way it is regulated, it does not give rise to a relationship between representatives and voters that may be a genuine relationship of representation. However far-fetched and inexact these theories may be, this does not mean that they do not contain a great deal of truth. Basically, the representative democratic principle has only been attributed a negative value. In other words, it has been contrasted with the royal and aristocratic principle to deny that the people can be subject to one person or a few people. However, its positive side has always remained in the shadows. One cannot disagree with the correct observation that the existing electoral systems are shallow devices, preferable to the system of drawing lots adopted in some ancient democracies, for instance, by the Athenian one, but still falling short of the purpose they are intended to serve. The so-called will of the people is unlikely to find its faithful oracle in the parliament, when the elected are, in the time between elections, independent of their electors; when both the various unsuccessful mechanisms devised for this purpose and the simpler but more empirical system of sorting the people into constituencies fails to achieve an organic representation of minorities; finally, when the representatives are thousands of people randomly grouped together, but distinct in their way of thinking, interests, culture, and therefore in their divergent wills. As a witty writer has correctly observed, the more enlightened the electorate, the more the civic and political consciousness of individuals develops; the more civilization, in other words, increases, the less likely for the elected ones to represent such non-homogeneous and numerous groups of individuals. The composition of the elected chambers, then, has something extremely artificial and fictitious. In the meantime one can hardly deny that a whole series of causes, the most varied, have given the people a political force, which is increasing more and more: the improved economic conditions, the spread of public opinion and of the critical and inquiring spirit, the expansion of culture, the daily press, the easiness of meeting and associating, the contacts brought about by modern industrial work, which gathers the workers around the machines, the speed of communications, which has abolished sedentary lifestyles and has become a powerful means of proximity. Thus, it often happens that the press and other energetic manifestations of social forces pre-empt the parliamentary forum and the activity of the parties and exert a far greater influence on the legislative than the former. And it is true that, alongside the forms of legal and political responsibility of the government, independently of them and with greater practical effectiveness, a kind of social responsibility of the ministers has surfaced. By dispensing with parliament, this responsibility brings the people and the government into direct contact. The existence itself of an unofficial press is something that may be deplored, and yet it can serve precisely to highlight this extra-legal side of public life today.

Therefore, the crisis of the existing state can be said to be characterized by the convergence of these two phenomena, one of which necessarily intensifies the other. First, the progressive organization of society around particular interests, which is increasingly effacing the society's atomistic character. Second, the deficiency of the legal and institutional means that society itself possesses for reflecting and asserting its own structure within the state's. And this deficiency could explain why even the associations and assemblages of individuals that, based on their nature and interests, should not take sides against the state, sometimes tend to make common cause with those that advocate

64   *The Modern State and its Crisis*

a radical and revolutionary transformation of public powers. Because of this, among other things, a certain distrust – which one cannot help but consider as extremely harmful – is spreading against the possibility of finding in the institutions created by the state and encompassed within its order the heroic remedy that is being sought. And it is curious and interesting to note that if by coincidence the sympathies and hopes of many converge on an institution [istituto], these people form the opinion that this institution is contrary to the principles of the modern state, even when it is blatantly untrue. Thus, for example, I do not know and do not wish to investigate here whether political representation can be renewed and can achieve its purpose by means of the so-called representation of interests. This system, at least at first sight, seems to correspond to the growing division of our society into classes and corporations, and would certainly bring back the ancient institution to its origins and primitive meaning. But people commonly point out that this would imply attributing a fraction of sovereignty to each group or class, and that it [the representation of interests] is therefore by its very nature incompatible with the principle that unifies and unites all public powers in the state. While its opponents deploy this argument to oppose it, some of its advocates complacently seize on this claimed incompatibility to develop and promote their anti-state ideas. The truth, however, seems to lie elsewhere. Leaving aside the practical difficulty of reconciling the particular interests of each group with the general ones, the representation of the former is as at variance with the defence of the latter as the existing division into constituencies negates the unity of the state and the organic nature of its interests. Recently, an idea already advanced by Stuart Mill has been brought back to the fore, that is, the idea of setting up a series of special parliaments for each branch of the legislation directly relating to this or that social group. And while some would like to attribute to them mere consultative functions, others believe that these new bodies should possess a real legislative competence, which would naturally narrow down that of the central Parliament, whose activity would be that of exercising control, especially in the forms of approval and veto. Still others propose that we should leave the elective Chamber as it is, or even modify it with the system of minority representation, and should rather reform the Senate by making it a Chamber whose members would be elected by professional bodies.

But whatever the ideas one entertains on these proposals that, in the ferment of the present, flourish and alternate, one principle looks to me as more and more demanding and indispensable: the principle that of a superior organization which may unite, conciliate, and harmonize

The Modern State and its Crisis 65

the smaller organizations that make up the former. And this superior organization can and will be for a long time to come, the modern state, which will be able to preserve almost intact its current figure. By its very nature, the modern state is not the instrument of a class, as some believe, a monstrous hypocrisy covering up the domination of a bigger or smaller number of people, an illusion before which, as Nietzsche would have it, only the short-sighted are allowed to kneel. Whatever may be said to the contrary, the state arose for the opposite end. Hence, it has the potentiality of asserting itself as an organism that transcends partial and contingent interests, that asserts a will that may well be considered general. In any case, the state is the only institution [istituto] among those that humanity has known so far that is able to give life to a political order which prevents the future corporatist society from returning to a constitution very similar to the feudal one. The greater the contrasts that will result from the specification of the social forces and from their increased and organized power, the more indispensable will appear the affirmation of the principle that public power can only be considered as indivisible in its entitlement – no matter how wider and more appropriate the participation of the various social classes in the exercise of this power may be. The state is not only the symbol, but the real entity in which this principle will increasingly materialize. It will become even more solid in its power and more active, the true personification of a broad and integral collectivity, which a transitory crisis may well depict as moribund but in fact is destined to acquire ever greater coherence and consistency. Certainly no one today can believe that our constitutional life has found those forms in which it can hope to settle for an indefinite period of time. New forms will emerge and many of the old ones will be transformed. But no one can seriously claim to know what lies ahead. We should limit ourselves to contemplating with a watchful eye and a feeling of faith the seeds that have already been sown. Naturally, not all the germs will bear fruit, but some of them have already taken root. And in the meantime, in those moments when one might be most perplexed by the formation and the opposition of contrasting elements, a conviction will come in handy: the good seed, sooner or later, will be fertilized by the patient work of those human beings who are not led astray by false illusions or selfish interests and thus have an awareness or an intuition of the high and pure ideals they are called upon to bring about.

Bibliography

Cammeo, F. (1898) *Lo stato d'assedio e la giurisdizione*, Torino: UTET.

Codacci Pisanelli, A. (1900) 'Sulle ordinanze d'urgenza,' in Codacci Pisanelli, A., *Scritti di diritto pubblico*, Città di Castello: Stabilimento Lapi, 96 ff.

Gamberini, A. (1903) *I decreti d'urgenza in teoria e in pratica*, Bologna: Zanichelli.

Gmelin, H. (1907) *Über den Umfang des königlichen Verordnungsrechts und das Becht zur Verhängung des Belagerungszustandes in Italien*, Karlsruhe: Braunschen.

Hatschek, J. (1899) *Der Ursprung der Nothverordnung: ein Beitrag zur Receptionsgeschichte des englischen Staatsrechts*, Wien: Hölder.

Lombardo Pellegrino, E. (1903) *Il diritto di necessità nel costituzionalismo giuridico*, Roma: Associazione per lo studio del diritto pubblico italiano.

Longhi, S. (1909) 'Sull'ultimo decreto di stato d'assedio,' *Rivista di diritto pubblico e della pubblica amministrazione in Italia*, 1: 137–155.

Majorana, A. (1894) *Lo stato di assedio*, Catania: Giannotta.

Menzel, A. (1908) 'Zur Lehre von der Notverordnung,' in Menzel, A., *Staatsrechtliche Abhandlungen, Festgabe f. P. Laband*, Tübingen: Mohr, 369–396.

Racioppi, F. (1909) *Commento allo Statuto del Regno*, Torino: UTET.

Ranelletti, O. (1904) 'La polizia di sicurezza,' in Orlando, V.E. (ed.) *Primo trattato completo di diritto amministrativo italiano*, Vol. IV, 1, Milano: Società Editrice Libraria, pp. 207–252.

Romano, S. (1898) *Saggio di una teoria sulle leggi di approvazione*, Milano: Società editrice libraria.

Romano, S. (1901) 'L'instaurazione di fatto di un ordinamento costituzionale e la sua legittimazione,' *Archivio giuridico 'Filippo Serafini'* 9(3): 3–74.

Romano, S. (1902) 'Osservazioni preliminari per una teoria sui limiti della funzione legislativa,' *Archivio del diritto pubblico e dell'amministrazione italiana*, 1(4): 1–31.

Rossi, L. (1894) 'Lo stato d'assedio nel diritto pubblico italiano,' *Archivio di diritto pubblico italiano* 4: 113–115.

Rossi, L. (1899) 'Il decreto-Legge sui Provvedimenti politici davanti al diritto e al potere giudiziario,' *Temi veneta*, 34(42–43):511 ff.

Spiegel, L. (1907) 'Zur Lehre vom Ursprunge der Notverordnung,' *Zeitschrift für das Privat- und Öffentliche Recht der Gegenwart*, 34: 497–536.

Vacchelli, G. (1898) *La difesa giurisdizionale dei diritti dei cittadini verso l'autorità amministrativa*, Milano: Società Editrice Libraria.

Index

Administrative state 4, 6
Analogia iuris 29, 33
Analogia legis 29, 33
Analogy 28, 29
Analogical interpretation 27

Bobbio, Norberto 1

Calabrian-Sicilian earthquake *see*
  Earthquake
Catholic Church 10, 56
Charles Albert 17
Civil Code 28
Corporatism 55, 56, 58, 60, 61, 62,
  64, 65
Criminal law 17, 30, 32
Customary law 29, 34, 35–38

Decree laws 2, 3, 11, 16, 18, 24, 25,
  30, 33, 41, 42
Duguit, Léon 56

Earthquake 2, 16,17, 24, 25, 27, 42,
  45, 48
Emergency 3, 11, 13, 14, 17, 18, 19,
  24, 35, 39, 40, 41
Emergency decrees 17, 19, 24, 40
Emergency powers 3, 14, 18, 35
Exception *see* State of exception

Fioravanti, Maurizio 15
French Revolution 9, 50, 56

General principles 33, 38
Giolitti, Giovanni 7

Grau, Richard 13

ius quo utimur 34

Jellinek, Georg 14

King of Italy, see Vittorio Emanuele II

Legal pluralism 1, 10
Legislative state 6, 9
Louis XIV 53

Mazza, Francesco 17
Martial law 27
Matteucci, Nicola 5
Military penal code 27–29, 33, 38,
  42, 47, 49
Mirabeau

Necessity, state of 29, 29, 30, 37, 38,
  41, 44, 46
Nietzsche, Friedrich 65

Opinio iuris 35
Orlando, Vittorio Emanuele 4

Private law 4, 30, 32, 51, 57
Public law 4, 5, 6, 8, 17, 47, 51, 52,
  57, 60, 61, 62
Preuss, Hugo 13
Private law 4, 30, 32, 51, 57
Proudhon, Pierre-Joseph 59

Ranelletti, Oreste 17, 30, 31, 36, 41
Rerum novarum 56

Index 69

Savigny, Friedrich Carl von 6, 8, 50, 51
Schmitt, Carl 9, 11–14
Sovereignty 4, 8, 9, 11, 52, 53, 59, 64
State of exception 11–14, 19,
Statuto Albertino 17, 39

Stuart Mill, John 64

Unwritten law 19, 36–40

Vittorio Emanuele II 7, 17, 39, 40